Criminal Justice
Recent Scholarship

Edited by
Marilyn McShane and Frank P. Williams III

A Series from LFB Scholarly

Prisoner Education Debates in Congress
Elite Discourse and Policymaking

Mark Tim Yates

LFB Scholarly Publishing LLC
El Paso 2012

Library of Congress Cataloging-in-Publication Data

Yates, Mark Tim, 1969-
  Prisoner education debates in Congress : elite discourse and policymaking / Mark Tim Yates.
      p. cm. -- (Criminal justice: recent scholarship)
  Includes bibliographical references and index.
  ISBN 978-1-59332-490-2 (hardcover : alk. paper)
  1. Prisoners--Education--United States. I. Title.
  HV8875.Y37 2012
  365'.6660973--dc23

                                        2011046885

ISBN 978-1-59332-490-2

Printed on acid-free 250-year-life paper.

Manufactured in the United States of America.

Table of Contents

Acknowledgements

First and foremost, I would like to thank Jackie, Janine, Marcel and Montierra, who all contributed in special ways. Also Willie Euzema Sr. and Betty, Cindy, Willie Euzema Jr., Lillie and the rest were vital to making this project happen. To Rick Lakes, I give my deepest gratitude. Others who have helped me along this journey include: Sheryl Gowen, Patricia Carter, Eric Freeman, Steve Howe, Wovoka, Mike Goerling, Taka Ono, Claire, Allen Bowers, Thay and Jon Anderson. Finally, I must recognize all those I have known whose lives have been impacted by the prison system, and who have helped with this study including: D., T., M. and J. This work is for you.

CHAPTER 1

Introduction

America, the "land of the free, home of the brave" has become neither. With over two million prisoners, our country has the distinction of the highest incarceration rate in the world with low income Americans hit particularly hard (Glaze, 2010; Warren, 2008). Massive incarceration has a rippling effect on these communities, resulting in families being torn apart and damaged lives (Boudin & Zeller-Berkman, 2010; Seymour, 2001). Politicians apparently do not have the courage to critically examine the causes of the penal state beyond a simplistic equation that factors in crime rates and prison rates. Prisoner education programs have a proven efficacy in reducing recidivism (Erisman & Contardo, 2005; Hrabowski & Robbi, 2002) and advancing the possibility of an inclusive, democratic citizenry (Davidson, 1995; LeBel, 2009). Yet support for education programs for prisoners has diminished in the past decade (Ubah, 2004; Coley & Barton, 2006). Only about 13% of U.S. prisoners have post-secondary schooling, compared with 48% of the overall population, even though most of the women and men in prison have finished high school or have an equivalent diploma (Harlow, 2003). When the U.S. Congress passed legislation in 1994, barring prisoners from obtaining Pell Grants, there was a decrease in the number of inmate college-level courses (Harlow, 2003; Ubah, 2004).

The focus of this work is an examination of reasons why prisoners are provided few meaningful educational opportunities while incarcerated. This study seeks to understand the genealogy of prisoner education policy through an examination of the debate surrounding the 1994 Omnibus Crime Bill and its prohibition of Pell Grants for prisoners, as well as the 2008 Second Chance Act and its re-entry programs. The study analyzes the ideological underpinnings of key decision makers and how their values are often embedded in the narratives of neoliberalism. In addition, the work examines elite stakeholders' discursive attempts, both manifest and subtle, to influence and maintain social policy through the creation of legitimizing myths, including the viewpoints that prisoners are hopelessly flawed or that they have potential only as human capital. Counter-hegemonic discourse is also described. The study methods are critical discourse analysis which looks at the ways text and talk maintain inequities in society and critical policy analysis. Utilizing transcripts from legislative debates, the study analyzes the discourses of members of Congress to expose the tropes that often lie beneath the surface of the debate over prisoner education. Their rhetoric appears to generate and maintain widespread support for legislation that is frequently deleterious to marginalized out-groups. The study should add to the literature examining the role of legitimizing myths that maintain inequities in educational access.

Paulo Friere states that education has the potential to change "the reality by which they are oppressed" by assigning "the people a fundamental role in the transformation process" (Friere, 1970, p. 126). But without a commitment to funding for the education of prisoners there is little hope of emancipation for many of America's 2.3 million prisoners. Over two thirds of ex-inmates end up back in prison (U.S. Deptartment of Justice, 2008).

The push toward mass incarceration must be understood in the context of broader economic and social changes that are embedded in neoliberal theory. Neoliberalism advocates free markets, privatization and a limited role for government in regulating commerce (Harvey, 2005). At the heart of neoliberalism is the view that an individual is defined by his or her relationship to the market. Yet, as Peter Kelly (2006) has pointed out, while the market itself is relatively free, the individuals within the market become highly vulnerable to manipulation. The effects of neoliberalism include globalization of the labor market, transformation of the social contract, and oppression of low-income communities. Neoliberalism has led to national criminal justice policies characterized by a laissez-faire attitude toward compassion and rehabilitation through education for prisoners. Consequently, mass incarceration has primarily served as a means to warehouse those most affected by economic changes (Wacquant, 2001; Western & Becket, 1999). Bernard Harcourt (2011) refers to this harsh criminal justice policy as *neoliberal penality*. The most egregious aspect of this policy is that teens or even pre-teens are often treated as adult offenders. Justification has taken the form of rhetoric that valorizes individual responsibility over collective action, and offers little in the way of a second chance for young people who deviate from prescribed norms. Massive expenditures that are necessary for the establishment of a police and penal state require the approval or complacency of the citizenry. Public sanction was gained through legitimizing myths such as those embedded in political demagoguery and the media sensation of a "war on crime."

Background

Of the over 9 million people imprisoned worldwide, 2.3 million are in the United States (Walmsley, 2009). Approximately two thirds of U.S. prisoners are African American or Hispanic (Stern, 2006). A report released by the Pew Charitable Trust indicates that 1 in 9 African American men between the ages of 20 and 34 are imprisoned. This compares with 1 in 30 for all men in the same age group (Warren, 2008). According to Michael Tonry (2002), disparities can be attributed to anti-crime politicizing that can be seen as a not so veiled pandering to race- and class-based bias. Both Republicans and Democrats add to the disparity by promoting 'tough on crime' policies that disproportionately affect people of color.

Life in prison can be paradoxical, with long periods of mind-numbing inactivity punctuated by occasional bursts of extreme violence. From the moment those accused of crimes enter the judicial system, they are usually under the constant threat of sexual assault and other forms of violence. While most prisoners are sentenced for non-violent crimes, they usually find a very dangerous place upon arrival. The violence is often under tacit or even explicit approval of the authorities, whose charge is to protect prisoners from violation. One prisoner recounts his feelings upon entering prison for the first time: "Walking into that penitentiary corridor is like driving the freeway ramp in the opposite direction of traffic, it is like speeding head-first into an onslaught of danger" (Santos, 2006, p. 22).

Some prison systems' answer to violence has been the establishment of "supermax" facilities in which prisoners are kept in isolation in cells, often six foot by ten foot that also must accommodate a toilet and bed. Prisoners spend up to twenty-three hours a day in their cells with an hour for exercise. In this environment, they stay for days or even years on end (Henningsen, Johnson, & Wells, 2010). Isolation, which formerly was utilized for the most heinous of rule infractions due to its psychological effect on prisoners, has now become routine in many institutions. One psychiatrist describes the effect of the lack of human contact on the inmates, "There is a general agreement today in the scientific community that the stress of segregation is the larger cause of high incidence rates of mental disorders amongst prisoners" (Irwin, 2005, p. 143). According to the Department of Justice, about 1.25 million of the nation's 2 million inmates suffer from mental illness (Stephey, 2007). With decreased social services on the outside, prisons became *de facto* institutions for low income people with mental illness (Blomberg & Lucken, 2010).

Harsh criminal sentencing combined with disparities in sentencing (Stern, 2006), and racial profiling (Sexton, 2007) have created a storm that has rolled over African American and Hispanic communities. Studies indicate that 50 percent of youth correctional residents have a close family member in prison. Lifting a member out of a family and locking that person away for long periods is comparable to dropping a bomb on the life of not only the prisoner but also on the lives of the family members who no longer have the financial and emotional support. The effects on all children of incarcerated parents can include "school problems, fear, anxiety, anger, sadness and guilt" (Sokoloff, 2007, p. 84).

Why We Should Care

Just as children bear the brunt of most wars, it has been so with the War on Crime. There are about 1.7 million children in the United States with one or both parents in prison (Glaze & Muruchak, 2010). By extrapolating to include parents in local jails, the number of children with incarcerated parents is probably closer to 2.3 million. In California, nine percent of the population under the age of 18 has a mother or father in the criminal justice system (Simmons, 2003). A

City Mayors Society report estimates that as many as 10 million children in America have one or more parents who had been incarcerated in their lifetime (Favro, 2007). In addition, the numbers have been trending upward in recent years (Graham, Harris & Carpenter, 2010). African-Americans are disproportionately represented among America's children of inmates. The Justice Department states that about half of the children with imprisoned parents are African American. Approximately one out of every ten African American children has a parent in prison (Glaze & Muruchak, 2010).

Children have been slammed by U.S. prison policy. Having a parent locked away can seem like the literal death of that parent to a child. One study of 30 families, each with an imprisoned father, indicated that 80% of the children displayed behaviors that matched those of children in bereavement. Compounding the sense of bereavement, the children often experience a feeling of guilt over the loss of the parent. Some believe that they were to blame for the crime and separation. "He'll come out and do it again and maybe it'll be my fault because he thinks he has to make a lot of money to buy things for me" said one child (Boswell & Wedge, 2002, p.62). Other emotions typically experienced include sadness, grief, depression, shame, anxiety, fear and anger (Simmons, 2003). There also can be the experience of being stereotyped such as one boy who was told "you're going to be just like your mother... a crackhead" (Boudin & Zeller-Berkman, 2010, p.88). In a recent report, Allard & Greene (2011) state that having an incarcerated parent puts children in the position of having to take on the role of adult before being developmentally ready. This is a heavy load to carry for a young child, particularly when taking into account the other burdens that most children of a prisoner carry such as poverty and the accompanying limited access to counseling and other mental health services.

Research indicates that children of inmates tend to do poorly in school with both academic scores and behavior suffering (Johnston, 1995). The educational decline found in these children may relate to a number of factors, including the emotional issues described above, social stigma of having a parent imprisoned, and dislocation. About three fourths of children with imprisoned mothers stay with someone other than their father. They live with either a grandparent, friends of the family, or in a foster care home. These arrangements are often impermanent and can lead to further emotional duress and declining school performance (Seymour, 2001).

Compounding the problems facing families with an imprisoned parent is the loss of a wage-earner. This is particularly harsh given the already low-income status of a majority of these families. Most people sentenced to prison are not high-living gang bangers or drug kingpins. Three fourths of state prisoners derived their income, prior to imprisonment, from legal activities. In addition, over half of male prisoners provided the primary income to their families before incarceration, albeit at low wages (Glaze & Muruchak, 2010). The loss of this income has a profound effect on families already in financial straits (Mumola, 2000). Chung and McFadden (2010) have reported that these problems are compounded, in neighborhoods with high incarceration rates, by a disruption of social networks and a relative decrease in volunteer associations.

Given the circumstances many children of prisoners find themselves in -- emotional anguish, dislocation, and extreme poverty-- it is not surprising that they often follow their parents to prison. A major study of children of prisoners found that 29% of those between the ages of 11 and 14 had been arrested or incarcerated (Golden, 2005). Bloom (1995) asserts that the "criminal justice system is intergenerational and that the children of incarcerated parents may be at greater risk than their peers for future involvement with the criminal justice system... the impact of incarceration becomes a multigenerational problem that must be addressed within this context" (p. 28). In the years since these words were written, it appears that the problem was "addressed." However, it was not done in a way that would reduce multigenerational incarceration but in a manner that would potentiate it. The rise in mandatory sentencing has resulted in a prison population that is younger than ever before because judges have less discretion to decrease the sentence due to the person's age. Mandatory sentencing has also hamstrung judges' ability to consider extenuating circumstances such as the person's role as caretaker in the family. It does not matter whether someone is the primary wage earner or the sole caregiver for young children. The judge often has little authority to move beyond strict sentencing guidelines once there is a conviction (Mauer, 2006). Mandatory sentencing of mothers is particularly hard on children. When mothers are sent to prison, the children stay with the father only 28% of the time. They usually go to extended family, friends or to foster care (Mumola, 2000). This dislocation can result in siblings being parceled out to different locations, thus completing the disintegration of the nuclear family.

According to the Urban Institute, about 58% of the children are under the age of 10 – a time of life when close parenting is imperative. Separation at this age often results in impaired socio-emotional development, traumatic stress reactions, developmental regressions and poor self-concept (Travis, McBride & Solomon, 2005).

Imprisoned mothers, because they are much more likely than fathers to be the primary caregiver, are hit hard by the prison system. One of the consequences of fewer U.S. women prisoners than men is that there are far fewer women's prisons. As a result, women tend to be placed in institutions that are significantly further from their homes than are men. The Urban Institute puts the average distance at 100 miles for male inmates and 160 miles for females (Travis, McBride & Solomon, 2005). With about half of incarcerated mothers living 160 miles or more from their children, it is understandable why 54% of state female prisoners never receive visits from their children (Mumola, 2000). There is more than logistics involved in the lack of contact; mothers may refuse to see their children. Bloom (1995) states: "The extent of powerlessness experienced by some mothers who are separated from their children is so severe that they sever their emotional ties from their children out of sheer self-preservation" (p. 25). Emotional detachment from their loved ones may provide a needed short term coping mechanism while behind bars, but it does not bode well for the mothers' future well-being, suggests Stephanie Covington (2003). The researcher states "The only source of hope and motivation for many women during their involvement with the criminal justice system and their transition back to the community is a connection with their children" (p.77). The impact of imprisonment on families can linger even after release due to the trauma of separation.

Children in Prison

Youth often are precariously balanced between the educational and penal systems. The nexus between these two institutions lies within the "zero tolerance" policies that have arisen over the past thirty years. Zero tolerance was expressed in the criminal justice system through the "three strikes you're out" laws. Such laws mandated life terms for three felony convictions, no matter how minor the third conviction. The attitude has bled over into the educational system with reports of "failing" schools that have become hot beds of violence, drug use, and other forms of social deviance. Within this atmosphere, schools have adopted zero tolerance policies that can result in suspension or expulsion for even relatively minor infractions such as carrying toy "weapons" (Giroux, 2006). In spite of the rhetoric of personal responsibility, zero tolerance laws have removed flexibility and responsibility from the hands of the individual administrators, and once again it is the children who suffer. Justification for this harsh treatment has taken the form of rhetoric that glorifies harsh treatment as, 'for their own good.' With sensationalist media reports leading the way, "the war on crime was brewing into a war on kids" (Chura, 2010, xii). The catch all phrase "at risk" has become the generic term of choice for youth, after which, the listeners may insert their own pet grievance. At risk for what? Dropping out of school? Low grades? Drug abuse? Sexual experimentation? Prison? Antiauthoritarianism? The possibilities are endless and often not explicitly defined.

Peter Kelly (2006) suggests that within a market-driven society, where self-actualization is located within a rational, productive and... above all economic framework, the goal of youth is to mature into the "entrepreneurial self." Self-improvement and responsibility are seen primarily as means to prepare for life as consumers and future workers. As adults, they exist as human capital to be exploited in the market, similar to a natural resource (Livingstone, 1997). For those who transgress this narrow path, the options are limited and include poverty, school failure and incarceration (Wacquant, 2001).

Over 100,000 youth are being held in custody in the U.S. They are victims of the harshest extremes of the new disciplinary regime (Muncie & Goldson, 2006). Young people have been vilified as out of control "super predators" by politicians, policymakers and the media. According to Michael Welch (1996), the "moral panic" created by the hysteria resulted in heightened expenditures for the prison/police industrial complex. He further states that the resulting state response does little to address the primary causes of crime, such as societal inequalities. In addition to the zero tolerance laws previously mentioned, there has been a cascade of laws passed that focus on governing youth behavior, including curfews, truancy laws, and anti-gang measures such as restrictions on assembly (Krisberg, 2006). These measures have had a two-fold effect. The first provides an inhibitory effect on what is a time of life that serves to test boundaries and find oneself. The other is to provide a legal framework for what Erica Meiners calls the "school to jail pipeline" (2007, p. 28). One of the primary links in the pipeline and perhaps the most radical reforms of recent justice policy is the concept that older children be treated as adult offenders. In the past twenty years, most U.S. states have enacted legislation that has lowered the age limit by which children can be charged as adult offenders. Only a handful of countries have executed prisoners in the past decade for offenses committed before the age of eighteen. They include such "stalwarts" of human rights as Pakistan, the Democratic Republic of Congo, Iran and... the United States (Muncie & Goldson, 2006). In the neoliberal paradigm youth is a frivolous, unproductive state of life, fit only for the human capital potential afforded business. Those that transgress the boundaries of this ideology are offered only the "pipeline" to prison, or in extreme cases, death.

Imprisonment has a multigenerational impact with succeeding generations more likely to wind up incarcerated. When we talk about adults in prison, their situations should be understood in context of their families and society. Prison has become a revolving door that requires a new kind of thinking to break the patterns that have become embedded in the lives of generations of families. Emancipatory education, facilitated through non-restrictive funding such as Pell Grants, can serve, along with other tools, to break these chains by creating informed and active citizens who are able and motivated to better themselves and their communities.

Justification for current policies come, in part, from political and media rhetoric advocating a "tough on crime" attitude. Politicians, educators and members of the media yield a disproportionate amount of power to influence public opinion through what van Dijk (1987) calls "elite discourse." This discourse has provided legitimacy to criminal justice policies that have been deleterious to large groups of people, particularly those on the margins of society.

Purpose

The purpose of this work is to examine why U.S. prisoners are provided few educational opportunities while incarcerated. In order to get at the root of the policy, it is important to understand the role of rhetoric and practice in creating the myths that provide legitimacy to current policy. These myths include the validity of the penalization of poverty and the hopelessness of prisoner education beyond narrow vocationalized choices. The study seeks to understand the genealogy of current prisoner education policy through: 1) An examination of the policy responsible for the elimination of Pell Grants for prisoners and promotion of the Second Chance Act re-entry programs and the ideological underpinnings of the key decision makers; and how their ideologies are embedded in the narrative of neoliberalism. These ideologies encompass a multitude of contexts such as economics, criminal justice and civic engagement. 2) An examination of elite stakeholders' often subtle attempts to influence and maintain the direction of the policy. These efforts can take the form of discursive efforts to establish the legitimacy of a particular policy within the eyes of both fellow elites and the public at large. I will examine these efforts through a process of critical discourse analysis.

Organization of this Work

The first chapter is devoted to introducing the problem of mass incarceration and the resulting fallout on communities, particularly those with high numbers of low-income families. Chapter 2 begins with an examination of the primary tool I used in this study: critical theory with a focus on social dominance theory. I then look at the overriding economic theory of our times: neoliberalism and its effects on prisoner education. There are contradictions embedded in neoliberal narrative and practice, as it relates to individual and corporate freedom and responsibility that have import for the inequities inherent in America's criminal justice system. Chapter 3 looks specifically at prisoner education, providing background for the congressional debates. Chapter 4 describes the process of critical discourse analysis as a means to examine the spoken and written word to identify the rhetorical devices used to provide legitimacy to current policy. In Chapter 5, the congressional debate over prisoner Pell Grant funding is examined to reveal instances of social hierarchy enhancement and attenuation through discourse. The Second Chance Act re-entry program debates are the focus of Chapter 6. In Chapter 7, I discuss the results of the debate analysis and their contribution to understanding the mechanisms for the role of elite discourse in bolstering popular consent for policies that maintain societal inequities. Policy resulting from the Second Chance Act debates will also be analyzed for its potential to provide avenues for either liberatory or oppressive prisoner education. In this analysis the questions I attempt to answer include: 1) What rationales are embedded in the neoliberal narrative that provide the ideological underpinnings for policies that deny prisoners education? 2) In what ways have these rationales evolved into policy? 3) How are these policies provided legitimacy through political discourse? 4) What processes are involved in establishing the legitimizing myths that result in popular support for the current prisoner education policy? Finally, I examine one possible alternative in critical pedagogy which could help empower prisoners so they could play a major role in the positive transformation of the communities they live in and their own lives.

CHAPTER 2

Prison System in Perspective

Critical Theory

This study utilized a critical perspective to examine the issue of prisoner education. Although the exact origins can be contested, Emmanuel Kant is often cited as a primary source for the development of critical theory (Rush, 2004). Kant looked at questions of ethics. How do our epistemologies shape our decisions regarding action? He suggested that reason alone is not sufficient to explain society. Kant believed that the way we see the world should be kept in a constant state of examination using experience, observation and rational thought. According to John Phillips (2000) "the critical project...sets out to establish irrefutable grounds for philosophy by subjecting all its existing grounds to the most rigorous and painstaking questioning" (p. 13). Theodor Adono and Max Horkheimer incorporated elements of the work of Kant and Karl Marx into a theory that challenged the key assumptions of capitalism. Whereas Kant advocated the constant reexamination of reason, many current critical theorists seek not only to examine the world, but also to *change it* (Kincheloe, 2008).

A prominent figure in post modernism and its influence on critical theory is Jean-Francois Lyotard who suggested that the ideas of progress, civilization and liberation are wrapped up in what he termed grand narratives. Governments and other elites seek to establish the "totality" of these assumptions regarding civilization. Examples of grand narratives can include Nazi propaganda suggesting Jews were subhuman, as well as neoliberal views of the supremacy of the free market and globalization (Milner & Browitt, 2002). It is the role of critical theorists not only to identify and expose these often widely held values as illegitimate but also to work actively to bring about transformation. A description of how these myths are used to legitimize hierarchies can be found in Social Dominance Theory.

Social Dominance Theory

Jim Sidanius and Felicia Pratto (1999) have assembled a multidisciplinary explanation of the ways human societies are situated in a hierarchal manner. They proposed that as societies became more technologically advanced, they became arranged in group-based hierarchies. Dominant-group(s) tended to have greater access to symbolic and material wealth, known as positive social value. Symbolic wealth includes titles, educational degrees, and business contacts. On the other hand, the out-group(s) tend to have factors that bring a higher level of negative social value such as poverty, poor healthcare and criminal records. Social Dominance Theory attempts to explain the nature of inter-group conflict by examining the processes that create and maintain inequalities.

It is important to understand when describing Social Dominance Theory, that there is a fundamental difference between group-based hierarchies which result from the member's social class, race, or religion, and that of individual-based hierarchy, which arises from individual ability or achievement. According to Sidanius and Pratto (1999), "This is not to imply that the power, prestige and privilege of individuals in group-based social hierarchies are completely independent of the individuals' personal characteristics and qualities. We only wish to imply that such achievements and status of individuals are not completely independent of the status and power of the groups to which they belong" (p. 32). This relationship between group association and achievement stands in contrast to one of the fundamental tenets of neoliberal thought: meritocracy, which suggests individual effort as the overriding variable in determining success in the marketplace.

Sidanius and Pratto state that there are three primary modalities for stratification: Gender, which manifests itself in patriarchal systems; age, in which children are granted less economic social power; and a third, which they term arbitrary-set system. The arbitrary-set system may be based upon class, race, religion, caste, ethnicity, and/or nationality. They also suggest that while gender and age hierarchal systems are found in all societies, and tend to be rigid, the characteristics marking arbitrary-set systems are highly variable and more susceptible to change over time. Examples include the Black/White and English/non-English speaking-related hierarchies found in the U.S., Protestants and Catholics in Northern Ireland, Japanese and Koreans in Japan, and the French and Italians in France.

One condition that serves as a determinant in the establishment of an arbitrary-set system is the degree to which the society produces a surplus of wealth that can be concentrated in the hands of a dominant group. The inequalities found in hunter-gatherer societies tend to be gender and age related. Those societies with more advanced economic structures tend to establish multiple ways of justifying unequal distribution of resources. Sidanius and Pratto propose that manifestations of conflict between the in-groups and the out-groups can be viewed as a means to maintain and establish the social hierarchies of the groups. "Phenomena such as prejudice, racism, stereotypes and discrimination simply cannot be understood outside the conceptual framework of group-based social hierarchy, especially within social systems of economic surplus" (p. 38). These phenomena should also be seen as part of an infusion of discursive practices, such as ideologies, doctrines and myths that historically serve to either enhance or attenuate inequalities.

Discrimination, either individual or institutional, is influenced by societal myths, such as racism, classism, negative stereotypes and meritocracy. Whether a person endorses a particular myth is determined by her or his social dominance orientation, which is shaped by group membership, gender, socialization and temperament. Other means by which subordinates participate in their own oppression include favoring dominant groups over themselves, self-destructive behaviors, and what Sidanius and Pratto term ideological asymmetry, in which the dominant groups tend to be more ideologically-driven than those who are oppressed.

Building on the work of Gramsci, Marx and Durkheim; Sidanius and Pratto consider legitimizing myths to be a crucial link between social dominance orientation and discriminatory acts. Hierarchy-enhancing myths include the meritocracy myth, divine right of monarchies, nationalism, racial superiority and nativism. The degree that individuals tend toward hierarchy-enhancing acts of discrimination is often predicated upon the level of belief in one or more of these myths as well as which myth is accepted. One of the primary factors that determines whether or not a myth is effective in perpetuating hierarchies is the level of acceptance afforded the myth by those who are oppressed. Drawing upon Gramsci, and the notion of false consciousness, the authors suggest that for hierarchies to be sustainable there must be consent not only from the dominants, but also from those who are subordinated. The consent of those who are oppressed is accentuated through the myths that legitimize the status quo. When the poor accept their condition because they believe that they do not "merit" success or because it is "divine will," they are actively participating in the establishment or maintenance of the hierarchies (Sidanius & Pratto, 1999).

I would suggest that much of the public support for harsh measures associated with the neoliberal regime and the war on crime, has been the result of legitimizing myths that situate prisoners as the perpetual "Other." These myths include the belief that society provides a level playing field for economic advancement, and there exists a fair justice system regardless of class or race. Belief in these notions helps to justify the idea that those who do not avail themselves of society's "abundant" opportunities and are imprisoned are pathologically immoral and they are solely to blame for their predicament. Thus they are undeserving of any kind of meaningful second chance to reenter society as fully engaged citizens with all the rights and privileges awarded the elites. Neoliberal ideology fuels the myths. It legitimizes a view of human worth within a discursive construct of "equal opportunity" within the free market. Through elite discourse the beliefs are disseminated throughout society in order to provide justification and widespread consent for oppressive measures.

The Economy

It would be difficult to provide an analysis of the effect of current economic policy on social programs such as prisoner education without an examination of the driving economic force of the latter part of the 20th century: neoliberalism. What is neoliberalism? Neoliberalism is described by William Segall (2006) as a reversion to the liberal ideas of the 19th century with its completely unregulated capitalist markets. The origins of neoliberal thought may lie in the Age of Enlightenment, but its current formulations arose in the so-called Chicago School of economics with the musings of University of Chicago's Milton Friedman (1953). The project is class-based with tentacles in all facets of society, including state, economic, religious and educational institutions as well as the media. The later proved to be a powerful tool in promulgating the tenets of neoliberalism. According to Teeple & McBride (2011), "In the battle of ideas, the forces behind neoliberalism made wide use of the mass media" (p. xii). Contributors include conservative think tanks and media outlets such as the Heritage Foundation and the *Wall Street Journal* (Peck & Tickell, 2007).

Neoliberal philosophy found adherents in various political circles, including Chile's August Pinochet. With guidance from advisors from the Chicago School, Pinochet embarked on a restructuring of the country after his successful 1973 coup against the democratically elected Salvadore Allende. Pinochet's example was followed by England's Margaret Thatcher who met with major success in dismantling that country's regulated economy and at least partially destroying the social safety net (Harvey, 2005). In the United States, Ronald Reagan's 1980 election brought a concerted effort to privatize many governmental functions, including education and transportation with varying degrees of success. (Harcourt, 2011). Reagan was adept at confronting the power of the unions initially by firing strikers and subsequently destroying the Air Traffic Controllers Union. President Bill Clinton furthered the neoliberal project through the effective dismantling of government welfare programs and an escalation of the "War on Crime." Economic globalization of the markets was a major "accomplishment" of the Clinton years through the negotiation and implementation of free trade agreements that restricted the signatory nations' abilities to regulate trade and protect the economic interests of their workers (Harvey, 2005).

The War on Terror, precipitated by the events of 9/11, provided George W. Bush with the cachet to expand economic policies both at home and abroad. William Tabb (2006) provides an astute analysis of the cornerstone of Bush's foreign policy: the Iraq war, which Tabb saw as part of a strategy to consolidate global power for a ruling elite. "The function of neoliberalism is to increase freedom for transnational capital from state restrictions… It may also be seen as a drive to control through the use of rhetoric of democratic promotion and the promise of economic reconstruction" (Tabb, 2006, p. 175). The last sentence speaks to one of the major dichotomies that exist within neoliberal thought. The idea of democracy through the reliance upon the decisions and needs of the people has not been made manifest in neoliberal policies. It is this dichotomy between theory and practice, as well as the neoliberal view of the individual that I will examine in the next part of this study.

Individual choice is emphasized in the grand scheme of neoliberal ideology, from its philosophical roots in the Enlightenment right up to the present day. The role of the enlightened citizens, educated and reasonable, has been a central component to the neoliberal way of seeing the world and provides the theoretical basis for a plethora of policies, ranging from economics and education to crime and punishment. Milton Friedman, in a highly influential article published in 1953, emphasized individual choice in the market. On the educational front, Friedman is considered the first to suggest the use of vouchers to provide "school choice." This proposal is seen as a means to move education away from a collective concern and toward a free market system in which individual choice can make or break the child's future (Spring, 2000). Of course, in this instance the individuals making the choices are parents, not the children, even though it is the youth that must pay for any "bad choices" that are made regarding school selection. This is just one example of many inconsistencies that come to play in the rhetoric versus reality. Another lies within the hallmark of neoliberal educational policy, the No Child Left Behind Act. Volumes could be written describing the inadequacies of this policy, which is centered on a market-based approach through school choice and micromanagement of conduct and curricula. Moral and academic standards are imposed that place an over emphasis upon choosing the "right answer" with little wiggle room for subtle vagaries (Lipman, 2007, p. 46). The thrust of the No Child Left Behind movement led Joel Spring (2000) to comment, "Ironically, choice in education might mean the end of democratic choice of ideas. There is no meaningful freedom of thought if everyone thinks the same things. If choice combined with national standards results in uniformity of thinking in public schools then democracy is dead" (p. 30).

Elijah Anderson (2001) suggests that the neoliberal climate combines opportunity with dire consequences for those who do not make the right decisions. In his case study of a young African American man who managed to leave a life of crime, Anderson couples his success story with a dire indictment of the system that makes the young man's story media noteworthy. "Success brings class mobility to a fortunate few. Yet their very success serves to reproduce or legitimize the radicalized class and status structures that continue to oppress those who either do not encounter the same opportunities or choose not to 'sell out' in order to achieve the dominant society's version of success" (p. 137). Those few who make society's version of the right choices are held up as positive examples with the myth that society does not play a role in effecting the individual's outcomes. According to Bauman (2001), "in our 'society of individuals' all the messes into which one can…fall is proclaimed to have been boiled by the hapless failures who have fallen into it" (p. 9). Yet critics of neoliberalism, such as Bauman and Paulo Friere are cognizant of the responsibility of people to work individually and collectively to right the wrongs found in themselves and society. "One must take advantage of every opportunity to give testimony to one's commitment to the realization of a better world - a world more just, less ugly, and more substantively democratic" (Freire, 2004, p. 8).

The Privatization of Society

One consequence of the neoliberal thrust has been a move toward privatization of many aspects of society. As previously mentioned, privatization of government services has been a hallmark of reformists both in America and globally. Education, healthcare, prisons, and other state functions have all been targeted for corporate takeover with varying degrees of success. Not content with privatization in their own realm, Western nations have aggressively promoted privatization in developing nations through persuasion and coercion via the influence of the International Monetary Fund and the World Bank (Frenkel, 2006). Electronic media such as the internet, long touted for its free exchange of ideas, has been threatened by monopolization. Free and/or nonprofit applications such as *Wikipedia, MySpace, Facebook,*

YouTube, and *Craigslist* have been courted and in some cases, bought out by media corporations for commercialization (Harold, 2007).

Government outsourcing in the area of criminal justice has led to a rise in the number of prisons that are privately run by corporations. As part of the "war on crime," the past ten years has brought a dramatic increase in the number of U.S. prisoners from 1 million to over 2 million prisoners. Ever mindful of opportunity, business interests foresaw possibilities for profit making in this largely recession proof growth industry. According to Michael Welch (2011), "Prisons are courted on Main Street, but also on Wall Street where industrial corrections has created a bull market – further evidence that crime does indeed pay" (p.509). Led by Corrections Corporation, the private prison complex has grown from being practically non-existent thirty years ago to at least 118,000 prisoners in private facilities (Sabol, 2008). Critics, such as Judith Greene (2002), have pointed out that these for-profit enterprises have been plagued with problems, "the private prison system as a whole is falling behind the public prison system in maintaining the basic human rights of prisoners to a safe and humane correctional environment" (p. 104). Selman and Leighton (2010) have linked this failure to a general paucity of accountability that arises from the lack of public oversight over private prisons.

Perhaps no other institution has such a long and cherished tradition within the free and public sphere as that of education. The United States has made access to education a key part of national policy. However, the system has come under attack in recent years by neoliberal policy makers and theorists such as Milton Friedman, who decried it for teaching "socialist values" and creating large and unworkable bureaucracies. Their solution is the privatization of schooling (Segall, 2006).

Public Education on the Skids

The state of schools in marginalized communities has long been problematic, but accelerated under neoliberal policies, where public schools no longer bear any resemblance to a refuge of learning, but have instead become racialized, segregated and broken. According to Leslie Sassone (2000), schools are little more than a weeding out process with the purpose of disciplining students to bring them up to "levels of performance that will make them docile bodies in the global capitalist system" (p. 392). But what awaits those who are unable to achieve adequate performance levels or refuse to submit to what Foucault (1995) calls a disciplining of mind and body? Through a philosophy that imparts primacy to the individual, it is easy to see the marginalized group's failure to thrive as a matter of just making the wrong decisions, particularly from the elites' perspective. Because the majority of elites are privileged with the resources to overcome obstacles, they (we) see the world from behind those rose colored glasses. Thus, when members of marginalized groups fall into poverty, the dominant group asks why don't they just "pull themselves up by the bootstraps?" Individuals are subjected to the full force of society's wrath if the wrong kinds of choices are made. According to Richard Sparks (2003), this makes sense within the neoliberal theory of behavior, which is informed by a view that individuals are a product of the decisions they make. A person who is raised in a household that values the rule of law and respect for their country and embraces these values will succeed in the market-driven society. For those who question the way things are, there is little hope for them. Thus, it "follows that it makes little sense… to counsel, treat, coddle or blandish those who misbehave." For them, there is little that can be done, so "those who demonstrate a persistent failure to comply, must be incapacitated or effectively supervised" (Sparks, 2003, p.34).

Education is just one front in the ongoing war on youth's collective experiences. Bill Osgersby (2002) suggests a massive and calculated corporate campaign exists to commodify youth culture in order to introduce that segment of the population to a consumerism that preys on many aspects of lifestyle, including street culture. According to Giroux (2003):

> As the obligations of public life are increasingly defined through the narrow imperatives of consumption, privatization and the dynamics of the marketplace, commercialism encroaches on all non-commodified public spheres. The first casualty is a language of social and political responsibility capable of defending those vital institutions that expand the rights, public good, and services central to a meaningful democracy. (p. 74)

One effect of these projects may be to narrow the collective lens through which young people see the world. They may become less interested in working for non-materialist goals such as peace, social justice and equality.

Eroding Welfare State

U.S. economic policies implemented in the New Deal and post-New Deal era provided an economic safety net for those who were in need. However, welfare has become the whipping boy for neoliberal demagogues of all stripes. Programs that have provided a thin lifeline for those unable to compete in a brutal market economy have been slashed under successive U.S. presidential administrations - both Republican and Democratic. Under the guise of "Reaganomics," welfare programs suffered a process of defunding in the 1980s that culminated in the bipartisan welfare reform policies of President Clinton and House Speaker Newt Gingrich in which a time limit was placed on state compassion for the poor (Navarro, 2002).

Through the machinations of the International Monetary Fund, there has been a globalization of welfare reform with denial of funding for those developing countries that do not meet certain performance criteria. These criteria often include reductions in public sector spending on healthcare and food and housing subsidies (Kolko, 2002).

The effects of welfare reform have been devastating. In the United States, 40% of those forced off welfare rolls remained unemployed for five years, with many of them left in severe poverty (Coven, 2005). Clearly, sudden immersion of the poor into the market economy has done little to relieve social inequalities. So why this attack on the welfare state?

Since the end of World War II, there has existed an implied agreement between the working class and the elites to provide some sort of economic cushion to ameliorate the unpredictable hazards of competition in the market economy (Jayasuriya, 2006). Neoliberals, however, have long opposed welfare as an unnecessary or even malevolent state function. They assert that the market is inhibited by policies that forcibly redistribute income (Navarro, 2002).

Opposition is not limited to programs that serve the poorest of the poor. What constitutes welfare has been expanded in recent years to include the mainstays of the New Deal, Social Security and Medicare. Calls have been made to "save" the systems through, of course, privatization (Du Boff, 2002, p. 311). The public educational system has also been lumped in the welfare state umbrella. According to William Segall (2006), opponents imply that "students are taught in their schools to become mediocre and await the benefits capitalists have created. This is the modern liberal school - reflecting a welfare society, expecting students to graduate from grade to grade regardless of their effects - that neoliberals criticize" (p. 199).

While neoliberals couch their opposition to welfare programs in a purely economic framework, other critics of welfare take a more nuanced view. Difazio (2003) has noted the link between welfare and state control, "the poor-especially those who receive welfare benefits - are ruled over, under permanent surveillance and suspicion and guilty until proven innocent" (p.162).

Low-income people serve a symbolic role within the market economy, a sort of cautionary tale directed to the rest of society. "The sight of the poor keeps the non-poor at bay and in step. It thereby perpetuates their life of uncertainty. It prompts them to tolerate or bear resignedly the unstoppable 'flexibilization' of the world and the growing precariousness of their condition" (Bauman, 2001, 17).

Treatment of the Subaltern

In societies that maintain hierarchies based upon race, class and gender, it is the marginalized groups, the subaltern, that tend to suffer the most from social engineering gone awry. According to Pieter Spierenburg (2011), the very basis of criminal justice is one of subordination.

> This is a crucial point. This element distinguishes punishment from vengeance and the feud, where the parties are equal. If there is no subordination, there is no punishment. The earliest subordinates in Europe were slaves. In that agrarian society, from Germanic times up into the feudal period, freemen were not subject to a penal system, but unfree persons were. (p. 5)

In the U.S., people of color have experienced the brunt of punitive policies (Gabbidon, 2010; Kalunta-Crumpton, 2010). Because Blacks and Hispanics are disproportionably represented among prisoners, families in those communities have been ravaged by the prison industrial complex. The obvious outcome of locking a parent away in prison is separation from the children. The majority of incarcerated parents live over 100 miles from their children. This distance greatly restricts the amount of contact the children have with their parents. Personal visits are problematic given the limited visitation hours. Families of prisoners usually are low-income and with only one wage-earner left, long-distance travel can be very difficult (Travis, McBride & Solomon, 2005). Long-distance telephone service tends to be prohibitive for prisoners, with many prisons supporting their budgets with excessive fees on phone calls (Christian, 2009).

Children who do manage to see their parents in person, are often subjected to a traumatic atmosphere. Mark, age 16, describes a visit to his father: "I hated seeing him on ordinary visits at [the] prison. It was a real shock seeing him in prison for the first time. I hated being searched and often had to wait an hour before being called in to see him. The officers were OK though I felt they looked down on me and I could see that some of them were bullies" (Boswell & Wedge, 2002, p. 71). It should come as no surprise that a majority of fathers and mothers who are imprisoned report that they have never had a personal visit from their children while serving their time. With the average sentence of incarcerated parents in federal prisons over 10 years, and 12 years in state prisons, the separation can last an entire childhood (Mumola, 2000).

Devastation upon these families and their children may have been avoided for many of them if it had not been for the so-called War on Drugs. Imprisoned mothers have suffered the brunt of the drug war, since they are more likely to have been sent to state prison on drug charges (35% of women compared to 25% of men) or federal prison (74% to 67%). In addition, 32% of mothers report having committed their crimes in order to obtain drugs compared to 19% of imprisoned fathers (Mumola, 2000).

There are over 66,000 female parents in prison (Glaze & Maruschak, 2010). Include those in jail and the number jumps to around 100,000 incarcerated mothers. Many are imprisoned due to a Drug War that is controversial for its disproportionate impact on the poor and people of color. By contrast, in many European countries, drug use is less of a concern for the justice system than it is for the medical field. Here in the U.S., the punitive measures resulting from the drug-induced moral panic have led to a flood of mothers and fathers entering the penal system. Class-related strictures have further threatened the poor's resistance to crime. The lack of a comprehensive health system in the U.S. has shut low-income citizens out of quality addiction treatment programs, leading many to falsely believe that they can find "help" in the justice system. Women, race and poverty are linked in the war on crime. Nearly 20% of mothers in state prisons were homeless in the year before incarceration (Mumola, 2000). Compounding these difficulties, is the signing of the 1996 Welfare Reform Act by President Clinton which put a lifetime ban upon assistance for anyone convicted of a drug-related felony (Golden, 2005).

In the aftermath of the War on Drugs, mothers and fathers have been sent to prison, resulting in collateral damage that has blown apart families and their communities already weakened by poverty-inducing economic policies.

African Americans have been hit hard in the past few decades on many fronts (King, 2000; Street, 2003). The period of U.S. history following the gains of the Civil Rights Movement, in many ways mirrors that which followed the Reconstruction era. Reconstruction facilitated relatively enormous advances for African Americans in the area of civil rights. It was almost immediately followed by a post-Reconstruction era marked by massive oppression that has been duplicated in the post-Civil Rights Movement era. In *Better Day Coming: Blacks and Equality 1890-2000*, Adam Fairclough (2001) provides a description of both eras that is startling in the similarities. In the former times, there were political demagogues who "cynically appealed to the worst instincts of the white electorate" (p. 15) while more recently we have politicians who "exploited the racial fears" (p. 323). In post-Reconstruction, "The rapidity and thoroughness with which White Southerners destroyed Reconstruction…left many Blacks stunned, confused and demoralized" (p.17) while the present era is marked by a "sense of pessimism" among African Americans (p.323). The 1890s was a time when, "Accommodationists believed that policies had failed" and Blacks should "focus their energies on self-improvement." (p. 20). Post-Civil Rights thinkers include neoliberal apologist Thomas Sowell who suggests that present day African Americans should not "place their hope in politics and government," but should embrace "self-help" (p.335).   Of course not all African Americans accept Sowell's view and many are actively engaged in the collective struggle for economic, political and social justice. However, there appears to be limits to what they can accomplish.   Michelle Alexander (2011) has noted that the recent trend toward judicial control of Blacks and other minorities did not abate with the election of a Black president.

In the 1890s, hysteria over a perceived crime wave caused by the newly freed slaves led to mass lynching across the South, but prison rates were much less than current rates. Today's hysteria has resulted in mass incarceration of African Americans. In both instances the roots of these "panics" appear to be economic, with the Southern Whites of the 1890s fearing the newfound economic and political power of the freed slaves (Fairclough, 2001).   In the current, neoliberal paradigm, leaders use the prison system to a greater degree than ever before to maintain economic order (Wacquant, 2001; Western & Becket, 1999). Michelle Alexander (2010) refers to the trend toward mass incarceration of African Americans as the "new Jim Crow." The central point is that every era in US history marked by advances in rights for African-Americans and other people of color (Emancipation, Civil Rights Act, the election of a Black president) is followed by a period of reactionary activities (post-Reconstruction, Reaganism, the rise of right-wing Tea Parties).   To understand the nature of these episodes of reactionary hysteria and their exploitation for economic purposes, it is important to examine the phenomenon of "moral panic."

Moral Panic

Societal outrage over perceived rising drug use and crime in the 1980s led to a so-called War on Crime. This phenomenon has many of the characteristics of moral panics that periodically grip society. Other examples of these kinds of events include concern over the corrupting influences of jazz in the 1930s, rock and roll in the 1950s and the hippie culture in the 1960s. Moral panics can be defined by the following attribute: They typically engulf members of society who are concerned by changes in the social order they perceive as threatening to their way of life. Parts of these changes involve a blurring of the social mores that had previously provided guidelines for making moral choices. In addition, these moral crusades tend to dilate and constrict on a temporal plane although the length of time varies from one incident of moral panic to another. Another attribute of moral panics is the tendency of politicians, the media and other elites to seize on the event to create a means to provide resistance to the perceived threat. However, the proposed and executed actions often have no impact on the root causes of the panic (Thompson, 1998).

A common thread that runs through many of the moral panics that have arisen in the past half century is the emphasis on youth. Curiously, they appear to be seen both as victims, as in the educational crisis, pedophilia and child porn panics as well as instigators such as the panics associated with gang activity and punk culture. In some instances, adolescents are perceived as both the perpetrators and the victims simultaneously as in the moral panics surrounding drug use and teenage sex. How the different players are perceived is often determined through the rhetoric of the gatekeepers of discourse. Goode and Ben-Yehuda (1994) call these players "moral entrepreneurs" who are appointed or more commonly, self-appointed, to the task of defining which behaviors are immoral. They also determine whether or not the perpetrators of those behaviors are considered immoral. These crusaders do not act as individuals, but as representatives of a faction of society with some interest in that specific behavior. A classic example would be the Prohibitionist crusaders of the early 20th century who tended to reflect and advocate the views of rural, fundamentalist Protestants who represented a relatively large portion of the population at that time (Goode & Ben-Yehuda). Of course, the grassroots fundamentalists probably would not have been successful in achieving their legislative goals without the help of politicians, the media and other elite gatekeepers of power.

Are there instances where grassroots activism is bypassed and moral panics originate from the top of society's hierarchies? Chiricos (1996) suggests that moral panics often do not arise spontaneously from grassroots indignation over a specific crisis, but instead result from a cynical manipulation of the masses. He points specifically to the War on Crime as an example. During the 1980s and early 1990s, the U.S. witnessed an increase in the number of poor people as well as a decrease in crime. Yet, at the same time there was a massive increase in the number of prisoners. Chiricos proposes that it was a change in discourse that provides the connection between the three. He further suggests that elite stakeholders, such as politicians and the media, are driven by ideology:

> Moral panic keeps the vast majority of Americans – who are 'doing with less so that big business can have more' – focused on ostensible dangers from the underclass instead of the policies and profits of the investors of capital, who are responsible not only for the growth of that underclass but the frustrations and anxieties plaguing so many Americans. (p. 121)

Rising poverty rates and increasing discrepancies between the races have magnified the differences between the haves and the have-nots. The middle class has also suffered in the free market so that the "interests of Wall Street and Main Street are opposed" (Schmidt, 2008, p. 1). Politicians have cynically diverted the attention away from economics by exaggerating various crisis situations, such as the "crack epidemic" and "gang warfare" that tend to portray low income and people of color as villains. Many of these situations have their origins in economic policy, set by the elites, that does not provide marginalized communities with the resources to organically address the problems.

Critcher (2006) suggests that studying the phenomenon of moral panics helps to understand the ways elite policymakers, such as the media, politicians and law enforcement work together to wield and enhance power. "If they all pull together on an issue, their power is truly awesome. Opposition will be swept aside in the urge to action, generally a law authorizing draconian new powers to deal with the problem" (p. 4). Thus the amount of power wielded can be enhanced through action directed toward the perceived problem. Goode and Ben-Yehuda (1994) call the concept that a small, but powerful group can deliberately initiate and maintain a moral panic in order to increase its power base, the elite-engineered model. "Typically, this campaign is intended to divert attention away from the real problems in the society, whose solution would threaten or undermine the interests of the elite" (p.135).

Moral Panic and the War on Crime

Barry Goldwater is credited as the first presidential candidate to campaign with crime control as a major part of his rhetoric. In 1964, in his race against Lyndon Johnson, Goldwater called for a national focus on ensuring law and order (Gest, 2001). The timing, perhaps not coincidently, was at the height of the civil rights movement. African Americans had taken to the streets in massive protests, mostly nonviolent, in order to secure civil and economic equality. Although the movement had achieved mixed results, White America and its privileges were under attack. Concurrent with his war on crime policy, Goldwater was also running on an anti-civil rights platform. He lost the election, but according to former U.S. Justice Department official Gerald Caplan, "The effect of Senator Goldwater's lopsided defeat was not to bury crime as an issue, but merely to transfer the official responsibility to the Democratic administration" (as cited in Gest, 2001, p. 5). After his election, Johnson was immediately put under pressure by conservative members of Congress to address the issue of crime. Pressure was particularly fierce from Republican office holders, as well as potential presidential opponents. Johnson, perhaps in response to these attacks and to provide political cover for his stands on civil rights legislation, increased funding for national crime control efforts, as well as establish the Office of Law Enforcement Assistance (Chambliss, 1999). Thus, Johnson set the template for Democratic policy for the next few decades: support for civil and voting rights legislation while simultaneously promoting the tough-on-crime policies that disproportionately affected people of color. However, a Republican replaced Johnson in the 1968 election and that was Richard Nixon. At a time when many parts of America were aflame with rioting over the assassination of Dr. Martin Luther King, Nixon took note of the success of avowed racist George Wallace in garnering White Southern support. According to Fairclough (2001), "Nixon shrewdly exploited the racial fears and resentments that Wallace had whipped up. Promising law and order, courting Senator Strom Thurmond of South Carolina, vowing to appoint a Southern conservative to the Supreme Court, and vociferously denouncing the busing of children to promote school integration" (p. 323). Nixon ran into his own brush with the law and had to resign from office. However, his linking of tough-on-crime policies and a "Southern Strategy" designed to court white voters, would serve the Republican Party well for the next twenty years as they made electoral gains across the South on both the local and state levels.

Democrats continued to take cues from their rivals. The height of their pandering to White Southerners came under President Bill Clinton, from Arkansas. Clinton, determined to win back Southern White voters to the Democratic Party, campaigned on a tough-on-crime platform and won election and reelection thanks in part to that policy. The legislative centerpiece of his presidency was the Violent Crime Control and Law Enforcement Act of 1994, considered the "largest federal crime control package to date" (Oliver, 2003, p.77). Around the time of the passage of this legislation, America was engulfed in a virtual panic over crime involving the use of "crack" cocaine and juvenile crime run amuck. Two years later, conservative educator, William Bennet provided an excellent example of rhetoric of that decade, "America is now home to thickening ranks of juvenile 'superpredators'- radically impulsive, brutally remorseless youngsters, including ever more pre-teenage boys, who murder, assault" (as cited in Potter & Kappeler, 2006, p.9). In this environment, the omnibus crime bill easily passed, despite such radical crime control provisions as federal funding for a massive increase in the hiring of local law enforcement officers, large grants to the states for building prisons and restrictive sentencing guidelines. In addition, the law contained provisions which enhanced federal support for capital punishment and "three strikes you're out" policies. The latter was a concept of providing a life sentence for three felony convictions no matter how relatively minor the third felony (Gest, 2001, p. 242).

Within punitive theory, those who commit crimes; however slight deserve punishment. This establishes a cautionary tale for those other members of a community who contemplate breaking from the norm. This philosophy was put into practice by New York Mayor Rudolf Guliani, who pioneered an extreme form of law enforcement characterized by the incarceration of people for petty crimes on the theory that it would have an inhibitory effect on greater offenses (Chambliss, 1999). His techniques were adopted across the nation, putting into practice the neoliberal mantra of severe consequences for minor breaches of personal responsibility. Once there was deviance, no matter how mild the mistake, there was no turning back (at least for certain segments of society).

The cumulative results of the federal policies recounted above, as well as harsh state and local criminal justice policies; are seen in America's extraordinarily high incarceration rates and the disenfranchisement of millions of potential voters, especially people of color. These low-income voters could be at the forefront of electoral opposition to neoliberal policies. Clearly, politicians have benefited from using rhetoric to stoke the flames of the war-on-crime.

Contradictions

Within the current neoliberal narrative, the rights of the individual reign supreme. As described by David Harvey (2005), a neoliberal state would "favour strong individual private property rights, the rule of law, and the institutions of freely functioning markets and free trade" (p. 64). This theory linking economic and personal freedom has its roots in economist Milton Friedman's work in the 1950's at the University of Chicago (Friedman, 1953). Yet, in practice, neoliberal policy has been detrimental to individual rights by establishing a disciplinary regime to punish those individuals who deviate from a narrowly prescribed mode of living. According to David Kotz (2011), "Neoliberalism has an associated ideology of worship of the so-called free market along with a denial of any positive role for the state *apart from its coercive functions*" [emphasis added] (p.3). Positive outcomes tend to await those who whole-heartedly embrace free market economics with its commodification of everyday life, while those who stray from the straight and narrow are subjected to harsh consequences. This regime is manifest in many areas of society, including business, the media and schools. Henry Giroux (2003) describes a: "corporatized model of education that cancels out the democratic ideals and practices of civil society by either devaluing or absorbing them within the logic of market... It also promotes institutionalized class and race-based forms of tracking and a culture of failure for those who don't have the cultural and academic resources" (p.79). This is a disciplinary system that lays claim to the supremacy of the individual, but in reality marginalizes *groups* based upon race and class. And like those who are forced into a kind of virtual ghetto, the students are not provided much in the way of support, but instead are set up for exclusion from the benefits of the market economy in this "culture of failure" if they are not members of the elite groups. According to Wacquant (2001), the system "makes a fetish of competition and celebrates individual responsibility (whose counterpart is collective irresponsibility)" (p. 405). Within the neoliberal narrative we are all participants in an episode of television's *Survivor* reality show, on a grand scale: Teams work together to set up the rules and perform elimination rounds to compete against the opposing teams ("collective irresponsibility"), but in the end, the final team starts eating its own until only one survivor remains to claim the grand prize (the responsible individual). And how does society view those who make the wrong decisions, those who end up in poverty or in the criminal justice system? Like *Survivor*, they are booted out of society.

Bauman (2001) suggests that people's viewpoints are manipulated by the narrative that places the ills of society solely on the shoulders of the individual. Within the individualized outlook it is easy to see the marginalized group's failure to thrive as a matter of individuals just making the wrong decisions, particularly from an elite's perspective. Those who don't have cultural and economic capital will not do well unless they are exceptional cases. These exceptions, because they are unique, obtain the spotlight in the media, and create a "common sense" view that if they can do it then why not every person within the marginalized group?

An example of the contradictions in neoliberal philosophy and practice is the Bush government's rush in 2008 to bailout the investment firms on Wall Street. The privileged get help while those with less cultural and economic capital, receive little. When members of marginalized groups fall into poverty, the dominant group asks "why don't they just pull themselves up by the bootstraps?" Yet, those in power do not seem to ask the same question of themselves.

Prison and the Economy

Recent changes in the labor market have dissolved some of the supposed benchmarks that serve to stabilize the work force in the post-World War II period. Secure jobs with livable wages and good benefits have become increasingly scarce in this era of globalization. Loic

Wacquant (1999) proposes the growth of the US prison system is linked to trends favoring free-market economic solutions and globalized society. Economic restructuring, over the past few decades, facilitated by free trade has left a dual workforce. It is characterized by knowledge based occupations dominated by the upper and middle classes, and a second group that is chronically unemployed or underemployed and relegated into jobs requiring few skills. Wacquant suggests opportunities for the second group became increasingly scarce:

> The new urban marginality is the byproduct of a double transformation of this sphere of work. The one is quantitative and entails the elimination of millions of low skilled jobs under the combined press of automation and foreign labor competition. The other is qualitative involving the degradation and dispersion of basic conditions of unemployment, remuneration and social insurance for virtually all but the most protected workers. (p. 1642)

The rise of "flexible" employment (lack of job security, low wages, few benefits) has fragmented the labor market so that even an expanding economy provides no buffer against widespread poverty. In the midst of a collapsed economy the consequences are even more dire.

Wacquant proposes that these changes have disproportionately affected people of color, who traditionally have been provided solace in public social services during hard times. This is not so during the current economic/political project for, over the past few decades these services have been slashed and restricted in such a way that the safety net now lies largely in tatters despite some attempts by the Obama administration to sew it back together. Wacquant is not alone. John Irwin (2005) states that:

> For politicians, who had devised policies or allowed and promoted economic policies that helped to create the new ghetto, the ghetto was a threat to the political stability of the nation. [They consequently] increased the prison populations, and devised a new system of imprisonment and parole system that managed, controlled and eventually disposed of a large

portion of the young males and a growing percentage of the females in the ghetto. (p. 238)

Prior to the rise of neoliberalism, government welfare programs cleaned up the inevitable complications of a free market economy. The gutting of welfare programs in the U.S. has resulted in the increased difficulties for women and men who have been left behind in the new economy. In addition, there has been a conversion of public assistance into a form of slave labor through the establishment of "workfare" where recipients are forced to accept low-wage jobs (Wacquant, 1999).

The role of social welfare in society is controversial. Conservatives and neoliberals tend to decry them for the limitations that are placed on the free market economy. They seek to "hollow out" the state to its basic functions so it does not run in opposition to the marketplace. Traditionally the liberal governments that arose in the post-World War II era saw welfare as a buffer against the worst excesses of the market. In their point of view, welfare is "a means of compensation or redistribution, to redress the vagaries and inequalities produced by the working of market forces" (Jayasurya, 2006, p. 10). On the Left, are the critics of welfare's role in maintaining the capitalist system by providing a way of controlling the subaltern. Piven and Cloward (1983) note that historically, increases in funding for welfare are often preceded by social unrest by marginalized groups in society.

In the political climate of the past twenty years, "compassionate conservatives" succeeded in defunding welfare programs, setting lifetime limits on enrollment (thus setting quantifiable limits on compassion) and enacting workfare programs. The latter has been criticized (Bauman, 2001) for providing an additional framework for marginalizing large segments of society into "workfare schemes" whose purpose is not to actually improve the plight of the underprivileged; but instead serve as a means to shunt them to the margins of societal and ethical concerns by reclassifying them as a problem "solved." This point regarding the removal of an ethical problem is important, for all ideologies thrive on an air of legitimacy and neoliberalism is no exception. The transitioning of welfare recipients from the "dole" to a tough job market seemingly justifies free market economic policies, no matter how harsh the consequences. Whereas before, an individual could turn to members of the community for support, now under neoliberal policies, low-income communities of people of color have become fragmented through the intense pressure of a variety forces. These include the changing labor market, the war on crime, and the collapse of viable social programs. In its place has arisen a dysfunctional space, one of alienation and hardship Wacquant calls the "hyperghetto."

According to Wacquant (2008), the traditional ghetto has folded under a combination of trends including African American disdain for segregation, the dissolution of the industrial workplace and their associated communities as well as the impact of reverse white flight which has resulted in gentrification of working class neighborhoods:

> The hyperghettoization of the post-industrial era can be construed in part as a retrogression toward the physical ghetto, a retrogression resulting in an intensification of exclusionary social closure, since it now combines racial division with class segmentation against the backdrop of deproletarianization without the compensating action of a canvas of strong homespun organizations. (p. 102).

Poor schools, crime, and poor housing remain: Social mobility has allowed the middle and upper classes to leave, taking with them many of the resources; such as churches, and the local press that helped provide local cohesion. Also gone are the opportunities for economic advancement.

A community that is fractured, alienated, and economically distressed needs help; but with the loss of community based support the only place to turn is to the state. Unfortunately, during the past twenty years, the state has, for the most part rejected intervention within the framework of welfare. Within the dysfunctional and morally corrupt ideology of neoliberalism, there is seemingly only one alternative, just one option to control the masses of the disaffected and disenfranchised: criminalization. Bernard Harcourt (2011) refers to neoliberal penality as the tendency over the past three decades by American administrations to dismantle social welfare functions while increasing their punitive activities. Wacquant (2008) suggests it was no coincidence that there was a massive buildup of the prison industrial complex at the same time welfare funding was slashed and recipients were forced into precarious workfare schemes:

> The atrophy of the social state and the hypertrophy of the penal state in the United States are two correlative and complementary transformations that partake of the institution of a new government of misery, whose function is precisely to impose dissocialized wage labor as a norm of citizenship for the lower class while providing a functional substitute for the ghetto as a mechanism of racial control. (p. 277)

He is not the only one to make the claim that restrictive crime control policies are often implanted in order to discipline minority groups to maintain societal boundaries (Mauer, 2006; Tonry, 2002). Rick Ruddell (2004) suggests that the penal system is just one method by which the state can discipline a restless population. Others include use of strike breaking techniques such as President Reagan's dismantling of labor unions and the recent conservative efforts to remove collective bargaining rights. These kinds of responses, along with the increase in penality have an inhibitory effect on the rest of society "by reducing protest, labor disputes and other types of collective social outbursts" (Ruddell, 2004, p. 151).

CHAPTER 3

Prisoner Education

With little apparent sympathy for those who backslide, it is not surprising that programs designed to give prisoners a second chance have suffered. As early as 1982, U.S. legislators began trying to restrict educational grants for those attending college in penal institutions. Charles Ubah (2004) proposes that evidence regarding Pell Grants efficacy in reducing recidivism, had little role in the legislative debates. A much greater impact was a political climate that was negative toward any policy that provided aid and comfort to criminals. Critics of inmate Pell Grants selectively emphasized a few studies that indicated that Pell Grants for prisoners did little to reduce crime despite the preponderance of studies indicating a negative correlation between education and recidivism (Ubah, 2004). The fight to end prisoner Pell Grants was led by Senator Kay Hutchison (R-TX) and Representatives Bart Gordon (D-TN) and Thomas Coleman (R-MO). These stakeholders represent an unholy alliance of moderate white Democrats and conservative Republicans who drove much of the harsh crime control measures of the 1980s and 1990s. The media fueled the moral panic over prisoner Pell Grants. CBS and NBC television networks ran prime time programs examining college education for inmates.

On television's "60 Minutes," one advocate for a harsh treatment of prisoners claimed "You can hear kids saying now, 'well, you know, if I can't make it, you know I can foul up and I'll go to prison and I'll get a free education'" (cited in Page, 2004, p.358). Ultimately, hysteria associated with the war on crime combined with political opportunism to overcome all opposition. The amendment to the 1994 Crime Bill disqualifying prisoners from receiving Pell Grants passed.

In the wake of the Pell Grant elimination, almost all of the prison education programs in the nation were adversely affected. Several prison systems completely eliminated their programs. A few systems were able to cobble together enough funding from a variety of federal, state and private sources to maintain their programs. These funding avenues were often sporadic and regionally dependent so that some states, mostly in the North aggressively worked to obtain funding for prisoner education while other states have largely absolved themselves of responsibility (Ubah, 2004; U.S. Department of Education, 2009). Consequently, one of the results of Pell Grant elimination is the increase in the inequalities that exist between regions of the country that commit to social services and those that do not.

However, attempts to increase federal support for prisoner education have produced meager results at best. An example is the Second Chance Act of 2008, which attempts to institute a broad base of support for prisoner rehabilitation including education, rehabilitation programs provided by faith-based organizations and the establishment of "re-entry courts" wherein judges would oversee each prisoner's progress. In addition to education and courts, the Second Chance Act provides small grants for other re-entry services. They include housing, employment services, transitional medical care such as a couple of weeks of prescription medicine and substance abuse treatment (Second Chance Act, 2007). The legislation authorized $165,000,000 per year (Eckholm, 2008), which would come to about $225 for each of the 735,000 prisoners released annually. This legislation will be examined in detail in a later chapter.

Why Prisoner Education is a Good Idea

Prisoner education can serve a variety of needs. However, one measure that is often cited is the ability to reduce recidivism rates. Perhaps the most extensive study was published in 2005 by the Institution for Higher Education Policy. The research found, in an examination of prisoner education programs in all 50 states, that the programs decreased recidivism rates among those released as well as increased their prospects for employment (Erisman & Contardo, 2005). Yet, this is not the sole reason to support prisoner education.

Should we be concerned about victims of crimes committed by post-release prisoners who are unable to find employment due to lack of education? Should we care about the families of prisoners who often face emotional, psychological and economic hardship because of the loss of a loved one? Most definitely we should, but what do we feel about the prisoners themselves, the ones who have overstepped the borders of society's moral and judicial codes? Criminologist David Garland (2001) describes two of the dominant schools of thought in criminology: 1) There are those who view prisoners as having the same opportunities as everyone else, but they made the wrong rational choices.   However, prisoners generally do not have the same backgrounds as most in society since they are usually poor with little formal education. To think of them as "the same as us" only with bad judgment is to deny the very real socioeconomic inequities that exist for most prisoners. 2) The other common outlook is to view prisoners as incorrigible, fatally-flawed "animals" who should either be locked up or released only under highly disciplined, supervised conditions, denied fundamental rights such as voting and free association. To dehumanize them in this manner is to dismiss the lives of former prisoners such as Socrates, Jesus Christ, Rosa Parks, Mahatma Gandhi, Martin Luther King, Jr., Eugene Debs and Nelson Mandela.

Garland suggests an alternative outlook, one that recognizes irrationality can be universal and that choices are usually not made out of context of the existent economic and social conditions. This way of seeing prisoners does not romanticize or demonize them. It allows us to realistically examine the societal conditions that give rise to our police and penal state; and to work toward equality based upon an understanding of our shared life struggle. Kevin Warner and Thom Gehring (2007) suggest this view can be applied to how prisoners are educated.

> Whether we are dealing with a prisoner in the overall context of the prison, or a learner who happens to be in prison, deficit models – which in each case over concentrate on what is deemed wrong or missing – are avoided as far as possible in favour of broader approaches to imprisonment and to education that recognizes the common humanity of our fellow citizens in prison. (p 182)

The Role of Prisoner Education

During congressional debate regarding Pell Grant elimination, members of the Congressional Black Caucus such as Representative John Conyers (D-MI) argued that since the purpose of the Pell Grant was to provide assistance to those in society who are of dire circumstances, there is no place where the need is greater than in prison. Even the old war horse of many congressional fights to secure educational funding for the poor, the man from whom the grants received their name, Claiborne Pell (D-RI), argued against cutting off prisoner access to the program. Other opponents of the legislation to eliminate prisoner Pell Grants included then Attorney General Janet Reno, the Federal Bureau of Prisons, and the American Correctional Association (Page, 2004).

In 1971, Supreme Court Justice Warren Burger (1985) spoke at the first National Conference on Corrections:

> We know that today the programs of (prisoner) education range from nonexistent to inadequate, with all too few exceptions. However we do it, the illiterate and the unskilled who are sentenced for substantial terms must be given the opportunity, the means, and the motivation to learn his way to freedom. (p. 193)

Prison-based programs have dated back to the 1800s as reformers sought to extend basic and vocational education, as well as moral education to those who had been convicted of crimes (Welch, 1996). Gehring and Wright (2003) propose that many of these early reformers were not just interested in improving the virtues of the inmates, but also had a sophisticated understanding of the anti-democratic nature of penal systems. They had the progressive notion that prisoners were capable of being agents in their own reformation by taking responsibility for education. Gehring and Wright call the presence of these early radical prison educators, "the hidden heritage of correctional education" (p. 5). They suggest that this thread of progressiveness extended up through World War II after which Cold War pragmatism resulted in a return to basic education (Gehring & Wright 2003). Much of the programs of the 1960s and 1970s followed a functionalist approach that equated an inmate's future success as a law-abiding citizen with the knowledge required to obtain lawful employment and negotiate legal society. These skill sets focused primarily on obtaining vocational skills and basic literacy. Howard Davidson describes this theory:

> It propounds that crime results from individuals making poor (i.e. criminal) decisions when faced with life's many problems. Out of neoliberalism comes the market metaphor, in which individuals make rational decisions based on calculating benefits against costs. (p.4)

How did the modern functionalist approach to prisoner education take root? Much of the impetus seems to have arisen from human capital theory.

Human capital theory plays a major role in neoliberal attitudes toward education. Human capital theory has been described by Robert Hart and Thomas Moutos (1995) as skills training for workers as an investment meant to provide dividends in terms of earning power for the worker and more importantly increased labor force for the market. The workers' skill sets are seen as a form of market capital. Human capital theory assumes that humans exist primarily to work. An examination of historic patterns of work indicates the idea, that humans are inherently oriented with the urge to fill free time being "productive," is a contrivance centered primarily in Western society (Sahlins, 1972). Although dominant throughout the industrial age, human capital theory obtained its greatest urgency during the reign of neoliberalism as it wound its way from its manufacturing origins into the corridors of education. Current school reform efforts reflect this orientation with the back-to-basics approach and semi-vocationalized curricula. Critics of a human capital approach to education see it as mechanistic and suggest it does not take into account the role of education in maintaining a vibrant, democratic society (Giroux, 2006).

Hartog and Oosterbeck (2007) suggest a human capital theory education formula can be derived in which a ratio of years of education to earned income can be predicted. This reductionist view of the role of schooling discounts exogenous factors affecting income level such as availability of jobs as well as racism and sexism and other forms of discrimination.

Human capital theory reached a high level of urgency in education among neoliberals as concern arose regarding the ability of the U.S. to compete in the international marketplace. Proponents included presidents George Bush and Bill Clinton through the Goals 2000 project which set the priority for education, to engender the workers who could increase the role of the U.S. in global capitalism (Briscoe, 2000). A centerpiece of human capital theory in education was the No Child Left Behind Act which narrowed the focus of content toward "back to basics" skills required for the technical workplace such as math, reading and science. This came at the expense of the skills required for a well-rounded life such as the arts, social science, physical education, and music. According to Pauline Lipman (2007), No Child Left Behind is:

> Explicitly designed to meet the needs and technical rationality of business... symbolically, as well as practically, national testing constitutes a system of quality control, verifying that those who survive the gauntlet of tests and graduate have the literacies and dispositions business requires. (p. 46)

Lipman sees No Child Left Behind as a disciplinary process destined to produce docile workers, the ultimate in human capital. Inmate job-training programs also fulfill this need.

A liberal arts curriculum became a major component of many prisoner education programs in the 1970s and 1980s, in a way it had never done before, in part because of the role of Pell Grants. Mary Wright (2001) states that liberal arts programs in prisons continued during the 1990s even as they fell out of favor in the larger world of academia. She gives several reasons, including the lack of flexibility in the slow pace of change in prisons and prohibitive costs of the equipment used in technical training programs. However in the 1990s, liberal arts had a decreased presence in prisons as adult basic education and vocational education programs reasserted their primacy (Wright, 2001). They included carpentry, electronics, painting, heating and air-conditioning and plumbing as well as computer literacy. The emphasis on job training spilled over into the math and language arts programs as they were retooled to focus on technical reading and writing (Steuer,2001). Between 1995 and 2000, while those offering basic education for adults increased from 76% to 80%, the percentage of state prisons offering college courses decreased from 31% to 26%. State prisons offering vocational education increased from 54% to 55% and private prisons increased from 25% to 44% in the same time span (Harlow, 2003).

In addition to the dissolution of prisoner Pell Grants, other reasons are given for the decrease in the number of prisons offering college level education. One is the perceived threat of liberal arts curricula to the penal system. Wright (2001) states that a "liberal arts curriculum, which often emphasizes critical thinking, intellectual and moral reasoning and development of an inmate's sense of self may pose a challenge to the established order of a correctional facility" (p. 13). Additionally, prisoner education programs became more dependent upon outcome based funding with the loss of the Pell Grants. Performance based management of these programs, like the parallel movement in public schools led to the "school report cards" that quantifiably measure the effectiveness of the programs in turning out their product (Linton, 2005). Curricula that apply to empirical studies, such as testing in basic adult education, had priority over liberal arts; which seemingly has more nebulous outcomes. John Linton (2005) of the U.S. Department of Education's Correction Education division stated that "The current climate [requires] that expenditure of public funds be restricted to 'scientifically proven' effective interventions" (p. 91). Job training fits well to this regime because the results of the program could be measured empirically through the numbers of the test group who are able to obtain work. In addition, recidivism rates could be obtained. Numerous studies have pointed to the inverse relationship between vocational technical programs and recidivism (Hall & Bannatyne, 2000; Gordon & Weldon, 2003; Young & Mattuci, 2006).

Empirical studies focusing strictly on recidivism as a measurement of achievement have not been without their faults. There is a tendency for the inmates to self-select into the programs. These participants were probably more motivated, as a whole, to succeed upon their release, than those who did not participate (Ubah, 2002). This brings up another important question: What about those who slip through the cracks in the empirical studies? An example may be found in Robert

Mattuci's (2003) description of the vocational program he set up in a New York state prison.

Mattuci's course consisted of eight sessions to teach the students basic plumbing skills in order to increase their employment prospects upon release. Mattuci, who had a bachelor's degree in education and twenty years of experience as a plumber, appeared to incorporate a well-thought out system of pedagogy. He relates that "many inmates have never known a positive schooling experience so they lack the needed confidence to succeed at learning something new. A key to the program is therefore validating their differences as individuals and accommodating their multiple learning styles" (p. 16). Mattuci had them work in groups for all hands-on activities and encouraged brainstorming and problem solving. Yet, despite the care in which the teacher took in order to facilitate a sense of community on the shop floor, there were a significant number of inmates who did not take to the class.

> Especially for the younger inmates, gang activity is very evident. The dropout rate of the male youth in three of the groups was 90%. For those influenced by gangs, there is a total lack of respect for the process of setting goals and working toward them. (p. 17).

A conventional vocational program may not reach this group of inmates who, as dropouts of the program are more likely to return to prison.

While recidivism is an important issue, it must be understood within context of the many variables that exist both within the inmates and, just as importantly, the conditions that exist once they are released. Barriers to post-release employment include lack of current job skills in a rapidly changing market, lack of available jobs in a tight market, the large hole in the employment history created by incarceration, and perhaps most significantly, the criminal record (Thompson and Cummings, 2010). With the rise of the information society, even jobs considered "menial," require criminal background checks. The perceived and actual impediments to employment can decrease the seeker's motivation and self-image (Pavis, 2002). Combined with conditions that facilitated a life of crime in the first place: poverty, discrimination, substance abuse, the deck is stacked against the average inmate. Conventional job training in itself is clearly not going to arm these people against the challenges of life on the outside. The attributes previously described that led some prisons to reject liberal arts education; the "critical thinking, intellectual and moral reasoning" leading to a "sense of self," must be cultivated (p. 1).

Friere (2004), Giroux (2006) and others have called for a pedagogy that is freed from the bonds of the economic bottom-line. According to Michael Kaiser (2010) it is more important that the student receives "a self-identified satisfying outcome, than to ensure that an offender who takes Program A winds up employed in Field A" (p.19). Mike Cole (2005) puts it succinctly, calling for schools to become sites where:

> Teachers, other school workers and pupils/students not only agitate for changes within the classroom and within the institutional context of the school, but also support a transformation in the objective conditions in which students and their parents labor. (p. 16)

In this vision, there is no room for docile workers. Schools would be transformed into emancipatory institutions where workers would not only be provided basic literacy, vocational skills and liberal arts, but would also learn to advocate for a better world. I explore this possibility later.

The Pell Grant

Recent trends in prisoner education have narrowed educational choice away from college toward basic job training (U.S. Department of Education, 2009). One event that facilitated this process was the denial of Pell Grants to prisoners. The U.S. Congress created the Basic Educational Opportunity Grant (BEOG) program in 1972 in response to the need for financial assistance for those pursuing post-secondary education. In 1980, the program was given a new title: the Pell Grant Program in recognition of Senator Claiborne Pell of Rhode Island, who was instrumental in its establishment. The original legislation specified a maximum award of $1,400 per year minus the recipient's expected family contribution. Thus it sought to keep the program within sight of its original mission: To provide the bulk of funding to those students who had the greatest financial need. Expected family contribution is computed by estimating the family's discretionary income by subtracting expenses from income. Assets such as savings, investments, real estate and businesses are also taken into account (Boren, 1989).

The Pell Grant Program is the largest need-based federal financial assistance program for post-secondary education. In 2005, there were about 5.3 million students who were awarded a combined $13 billion in aid. Despite the seemingly large amount of assistance and the rise in inflation-adjusted annual funding since the program's inception, the Pell Grant Program has met with limited success in adjusting to the rising costs of tuition. The average earnings of low-income families remained static from 1973 to 2005. Yet rising tuition has resulted in an average cost that would require 82% of a low-income family's annual earnings to pay for tuition costs compared to 43% of that family's earnings in 1973 (Cook & King, 2007).

Obtaining less bang for the buck has focused attention on eligibility requirements for participation in the Pell Grant program. A 1992 amendment simplified the needs test for the program by de-emphasizing the role of assets. In addition, the "60% rule" was eliminated. In previous years, the Pell Grant was limited to 60% or less of the tuition costs. This rule decreased the amount of aid that low-income students were eligible for relative to middle-income students since those with lower income tended to go to institutions with lower tuition costs (Schenet et al, 2003).

<u>Characteristics of Pell Grant Recipients</u>
Pell Grants are generally restricted to students who do not already have a baccalaureate degree, and are seeking a degree at a college or job training at a technical school (U.S. Department of Education, 2004). Despite the limitations passed by federal funding allocations and the rise of tuition and related costs, the Pell Grant remains somewhat true to its original mission of serving primarily low-income students. The median income of recipients was $17,217 in 2005. This marked an inflation-adjusted increase of only about $1,300 from 1977. Of those students with greater than $50,000 in income, about 4% receive Pell Grant funding while 78% of those making less than $10,000 are

recipients. The 4% have extenuating circumstances such as very large families, high medical expenses or other financial hardships. African Americans, Hispanics and Native Americans tend to be disproportionately represented among Pell Grant recipients who are attending post-secondary institutions. Students whose parents have no college degree are also more likely to get the Pell (Cook & King, 2007). Despite the focus of the Pell Grant Program on the needy, the ones who were most in need of the help were cut off when eligibility was cut off for prisoners.

<u>Why the Pell Grant for Prisoners?</u>
In this study, I focus, in part, on the debate surrounding the denial of the Pell Grant to incarcerated individuals. But why did I choose the Pell Grant? After all, there are numerous potential funding sources for prisoner education, including other federal programs, state and private funding as well as tuition payment by the prisoners themselves. However, for various reasons those other sources can be problematic for prisoners who seek a liberal arts education. Federal programs tend to be held captive to whatever political wind is blowing in Washington at the time. Recent emphasis has been placed on skills-based training for prisoners through basic education and vocational training. While these programs can be helpful, they may not address the needs of the prisoners who aspire to higher education.

In its most recent survey of educational attainment (Harlow, 2003), the U.S. Department of Justice states that about 60% of prisoners have a GED, high school diploma, or some college. Accordingly, over half of America's 2.3 million prisoners are considered academically qualified to take college-level courses for credit. While many are qualified on paper to take higher level courses – do they have the wherewithal to handle the academic rigor? A recent study by Harlow et al (2010) indicates that inmates who have GEDs tend to have greater reading skills than non-inmates with GEDs.

Prison educators often characterize their students as academically rigorous. An example would be Rachel Toor (2010), who teaches creative writing at the graduate level. She describes her introduction to prisoner education:

Last spring a student who had been teaching at a medium-security state prison asked if I would come to his class as a guest. He wanted to be able to let his students meet a published author. They were, he thought, starting to question his authority as a writer. I said yes without hesitation. The class surprised me. A bunch of the guys had college degrees, and at least one had already earned a master's. Many of them had been taking writing courses for years and were adept at deploying the jargon of our trade. They were astute readers, and some were good writers. I realized how challenging it was for graduate students who hadn't published themselves to have writing cred with this group. I decided to go back for more. (p.1)

Toor's class was atypical given her students' graduate level status, but apparently their thirst for education was not, even when compared to traditional students. Jefferson Cowie (2010), a professor at Cornell, compares his experiences teaching at his home university with those at a penal institution in the following two passages:

On the Cornell campus, every time I'd attended the huge opening of the reading project, I was struck by the students' indifference and boredom… the students seemed incapable of engaging with the lectures.

The 60 inmates enrolled in the Cornell Prison Education Program were, in contrast to the Cornell students, hardly bored, restless, or indifferent. They were on fire. They sat attentively without PowerPoint photos to keep them entertained, autumn walks through the gorges to look forward to, or fancy careers to anticipate. They occasionally tossed questions to me during my talk, testing my mettle. Then, when I finished, their hands shot up. For the next hour, I got a vigorous intellectual workout--an exhausting barrage of questions any teacher would relish. (p.B20)

Many prisoners have the credentials, the interest and apparently the acumen to take college courses, but few have that experience. About

48% of the general population has some post-secondary education, but only 13% of America's prisoners (Harlow, 2003). Yet, due to the de-emphasis of college courses in prisons, they are often denied access. After the 1994 Omnibus Crime Bill ended Pell Grants for prisoners, several states sought to take up the slack, either through direct grants to prisons or through programs administered through state universities (Taylor, 2005). However, this support tended to be sporadic and just as open to political influence as the federal level. Most states spend about half their overall budget on restricted projects, such as construction and services. The rest of spending is considered discretionary and must be reauthorized each year. The term discretionary is somewhat misleading since into this category falls such politically sensitive projects as university systems and the overall corrections programs. When economic times are tough and dollars are scarce, "non-essential" services such as prisoner education were often axed in the budget cutting process (Justice Policy Institute, 2002). This was one advantage of rolling prisoner education funding under the federal Pell Grant umbrella. The Pell Grant, since its origins in the 1960s, has been and remains a politically popular program, avoiding elimination or even severe reductions under the administrations of anti-social program hawks such as Ronald Reagan (Schenet et al, 2003). When G. W. Bush sought to eliminate other Great Society programs, including Upward Bound and the Educational Talent Search, the administration proposed that the savings be funneled into Pell Grants (Saks, 2007).

Therein lay a reason to return Pell Grant eligibility to prisoners. Like the 1965 Voting Rights Act, which provided a federal guarantee of ballot access that superseded sporadic state guarantees; persistent, nondiscriminatory federal funding for education of the incarcerated is possible with Pell Grant funding. Because it is a federal program that goes directly to local educational providers to distribute to students, it is not held hostage to the political vagaries that plague some federal programs administered by the states such as Medicaid, whose benefits can vary from state to state depending on the state's commitment to the poor.

It is not just the Pell Grant's role as a funding mechanism that makes it particularly appropriate for the education of prisoners. The Pell Grant has proven the program's efficacy as a means to facilitate an emancipatory education. How does the Pell Grant help achieve this? It offers a means by which prisoners can obtain funding for liberal arts education either through correspondence or through a local college that is potentially less fettered by content constraints imposed by the corrections system or other representatives of the State. Programs for prisoner education often take a conservative, back to basics approach (Linton, 2005; U.S. Department of Education, 2009). This can come at the expense of flexibility and innovation. The potential of the Pell Grant program to facilitate a certain degree of academic freedom in correctional higher education has been documented in numerous cases during that brief "shining moment" when prisoners had access to Pell Grants. I relay some of the instances in a later chapter. They share the commonality of a high degree of prisoner participation.

Summary

The first three chapters have provided background for the current state of affairs including a description of the War on Crime which has provided public support; and judicial mechanisms for the control of large numbers of Blacks, Hispanics and poor Whites within the prison industrial complex. If prisoners are seen as wholly at fault for their actions, then society is off the hook when it comes to providing beneficial programs, such as prisoner education. However, as David Garland suggests, prisoners do not comprise an Other separate from Us despite their flaws. There exists a common humanity. This belief should not only be cognitive-based, but also heartfelt. Once prisoners are accepted back into society (even as they await release), programs that provide a helping hand become an imperative. Prisoner education has the ability to serve as a conduit for the transformation of prisoners into active citizens who care for themselves, their families and their communities. However, the potential of democratic prisoner education has not been realized due to the nature of the punitive regime. In order to address the structures that uphold current policy, it is necessary to identify and dissect their origins and the means by which they are upheld.

Social Dominance Theory establishes the framework for an understanding of the ways hierarchies are formed within societies. Elite members of society both establish and maintain unequal status through mythmaking. Common myths in America include the idea that individuals are entirely responsible for their fates, and the disproportionate numbers of members of a specific race or class who are poor or imprisoned is indicative entirely of individual failings and not of a societal bias against these groups. Others include the idea that education for marginalized groups should emphasize job training at the expense of higher education. These myths are buttressed through a neoliberal ideology that provides intellectual and moral justification for policies that have devastated marginalized communities. Myths are constructed through discourse among and from the elites.

CHAPTER 4

Research Lens

Research always has political consequences.
(Bogdan & Biklen, 2003, p. 225)

This work examined the policy and discourse of U.S. Senate and House members as they debated prisoner education, particularly Pell Grant amendments and the Second Chance Act. The complete transcripts are available in the Congressional Record. I utilized the technique of critical discourse analysis to unpack the discourse, and attempt to reveal the policymakers' use of *vox populi*, nationalism, paternalism and other rhetorical devices as a means to provide legitimacy to their aims. In addition, I used policy analysis to examine how their actions bolster a broader economic agenda. In this chapter, I will describe the research process utilized for this work.

According to Hugh Heclo, policy can "be considered as a course of action or inaction rather than specific decisions or actions" (as cited in T. Dye 1981, p.2). I will use this working definition in this study for a number of reasons. First, it suggests that what policymakers deign not to do has as much significance in framing policy as what they do. When a legislative body chooses to ignore evidence suggesting that children can benefit from universal healthcare, that is as much a policy as creating and sustaining a national health plan. In addition, the focus on broad trends rather than specific decisions as policy helps to distinguish between the often contradictory minutiae of daily strategies and the aggregate effect on the public. In this study, denial of Pell Grant funding for prisoners is seen as a specific strategy, and as such is only used as a starting point in examining hierarchy-enhancing policies and their effect on Americans, particularly those citizens who are disenfranchised from the political process.

A highly influential 1962 article written by Yehezkel Dror is helpful in distinguishing between systems analysis and policy analysis. He suggests that in systems analysis, the primary research modality is quantitative with great emphasis upon cost-benefit analysis. In policy analysis, the main focus is on qualitative methodologies and "imaginative and futuristic thought, and integration of tacit knowledge" (p.254). By tacit knowledge, Dror refers to the intuitive understanding that comes through adequate training and experience. In addition, policy analysis integrates a multi-disciplinary approach to research, often combining fields such as social science, psychology and political science. Criteria for making decisions in systems analysis appear to be based purely on budgetary considerations. Policy analysis takes into account multiple facets, including social, political and economic (Dror, 1962).

Dror's distinction is particularly appropriate in context of the debate regarding prisoner education in recent years. As state and federal budgets have tightened under the increasing weight of bloated corrections spending, justice and humanitarian concerns have apparently taken a back seat in the deliberations process. Palumbo (1988) suggests that discourse is among the strategies that set and sustain courses of action. In this research, I have used policy analysis as well as discourse analysis to examine the discourse utilized by elite policymakers in debating prisoner education.

Critical Discourse Analysis

Critical discourse analysis arose out of the much broader field of discourse analysis. Wood and Kroger (2000) describe discourse as social practice embodied in spoken (talk) and written (text) language. However, like many of the definitions that are found in qualitative research, it is open to various interpretations. An example would be using the term discourse solely for the spoken word. Another interpretation of discourse analysis is the use of discourse for talk, text, and visual images and nonverbal movements that communicate ideas (Wood and Kroger, 2000). Critical discourse analysis is a term apparently coined by Norman Fairclough (1995). He describes it as a method of discourse analysis that includes analysis of the "discursive event" in a sociocultural context. Fairclough suggests this is done with an "emphasis... upon the determination of action by structures, social reproduction, and the ideological positioning of subjects" (p. 24). While discourse analysis has the potential to be viewed as ideologically neutral by its practitioners, critical discourse analysts take an actively ideological role in their work. According to Ruth Wodak, et al (1999), critical discourse theory practitioners "do not pretend to be able to assume an objective, socially neutral analytical stance. Indeed, practitioners of Critical Discourse Analysis believe that such ostensible political indifference ultimately assists in maintaining an unjust status quo" (p. 8). They suggest that it is the duty of the practitioner to "intervene" into sociopolitical discourse (Wodak et al, 1999).

Teun van Dijk (2001) views critical discourse analysis as:

> A type of discourse analytical research that primarily studies the way social power abuse, dominance, and inequality are enacted, reproduced, and resisted by text and talk in the social and political context. With such dissident research, critical discourse analysis takes explicit positions and thus wants to understand, expose and ultimately resist social inequality. (p. 352)

This well thought-out definition encapsulates my outlook on the topic.

There are several important questions van Dijk raises that are informed by the points described above. How does ideology drive the influence of symbolic elites? How do the communicative events and public discourse of the elite effect opinion regarding marginalized groups? (van Dijk, 1993). I will begin with an examination of critical discourse analysis, a crucial nexus between theory and praxis.

Nicola Woods (2006) suggests that discourse includes language and context. She explains that it is "the context that we bring with us when we use language; the context that includes our assumptions and expectations; the context we change (and which is itself changed) in our relationship with others, as we both construct and negotiate our way through the social practices of the world we live in" (p. x). According to Schiffrin, Tannen and Hamilton (2001) discourse analysis, like discourse has a variety of meanings to a variety of people, but can be put into three broad groups. There are discourse analysts who look almost solely at language use. There are linguists who tend to look at "anything beyond the sentence." The third group looks specifically at the ways discourse enacts or reenacts power relations. Discourse analysts come from several traditions including psychology, communication and sociology (Schriffin, Tannen & Hamilton 2001).

There are several attributes that tend to mark critical discourse analysis. One is that it is usually multidisciplinary (van Dijk 2001; Wodak & Chilton, 2005). It is this approach I have embraced as I attempt to integrate critical discourse analysis with policy analysis in this study.

Another attribute that characterizes effective critical discourse analysis is that, due to its relatively new status as a research modality, it should be "better" than other more traditional forms of research (van Dijk, 2001). Because it is not based upon the positivist forms of inquiry such as the scientific method, or cannot be quantified into an easily read graph, it is often perceived as being a bit "dodgy." Critical discourse analysis is a form of qualitative research. According to Robert Burns (2000):

> Qualitative evaluators frequently find themselves having to defend their methods because of the resistance posed by researchers who are ideologically committed to quantitative methods. The latter assume, out of context, that quantitative research, more rigorous than most qualitative methods must be the best method to use in all research. (p. 11)

Effective critical discourse analysis should attempt to explain discourse structures in addition to providing descriptive analysis. The requirement seems fairly self-evident in a method that analyzes social context (van Dijk, 2001). An example is examining how power relations found in discourse provide sustenance to social hierarchies.

In a 1993 study, van Dijk analyzed transcripts of legislative debates in The Netherlands, the United States, Germany, France, and the United Kingdom. The topics involved, such as the U.S. debate on a 1990 civil rights bill, or an immigration bill in Great Britain, could be considered racially charged. The rhetorical, argumentative and semantic devices utilized by the debaters to convert listeners to her or his viewpoint were analyzed. There were several kinds of rhetorical categories that were found in the discourse. One was Positive Self-Presentation, which within the realm of parliament, often manifests itself as nationalism. This is usually not the chest-thumping of a Mussolini or George Wallace, but is often cast in a more "civil" tone. An example van Dijk provides is from the House of Commons:

> I believe that we are a wonderfully fair country. We stick to the rules unlike some foreign Governments. (p. 73)

In addition to the obvious self-praise and denigration of "foreign" bodies, van Dijk put the member's rhetoric within context of the "tough, but fair" self-descriptions that pop up repeatedly in debates on immigrants or minorities. That theirs is a "fair country," is qualified by saying that they "stick to the rules." Van Dijk says:

> Firmness in that case is like that of the stern father, or the wise doctor, whose firmness only benefits his children or her clients. The addition of "fair" also suggests that there is no question of being too firm because fairness prevails in all directions. This paternalistic strategy is apparent in many parliamentary debates. (p. 93)

This strategy of attaching qualified disclaimers appears all too common in political rhetoric. We have seen it here in the United States in "trust, but verify" and "compassionate conservative." Van Dijk suggests that in the dominant narrative, those who are only fair or only compassionate run the risk of being labeled "unrealistic, bleeding heart liberals" (p. 94). The above passage from the parliamentary debates provides an excellent example of at least four rhetorical devices commonplace in the coded talk of political elites - the aforementioned Nationalism "fair, but firm" strategy as well as Paternalism. The last one being so subtle that only careful reading combined with an understanding of context makes it apparent. The fourth device is that of the Disclaimer. One kind of disclaimer was already mentioned. Listeners who may have hesitancy toward the "firm" aspect of the debate - such as tougher immigration laws or harsher sentencing - are placated by the fact that it is "fair," after all. The "firm, but fair" strategy appears to fall under the broader field of disclaimer devices. Other kinds of disclaimers can include explicitly racist forms such as "I'm not racist, but..." followed by a covert or not so covert racist remark.

Another device is Negative Other-Presentation, in which those who are marginalized are defamed in some way. Van Dijk provides an example from the U.S. congressional debate over a civil rights bill:

> Any honest liberal would have to admit that affirmative action has been a dismal failure...Instead of advancing the cause of Blacks, affirmative action has hurt the cause of Blacks. Why? Because racial preference implies inferiority. And this implied inferiority actually aggravates the white racism that affirmative action was designed to eradicate. This is why there has been an increase in racial incidents, for instance on campuses, around the country. (p. 92)

In this passage, both the oppressed and those who fight oppression are blamed for racist events. Once again, according to van Dijk, there is an attempt to cover racism and "blame the victim." Within this passage, the speaker deftly manages to provide a negative picture of the Other, while subtly painting the opponents of affirmative action as the real anti-racists, as opposed to the congressional proponents of the civil rights bill. Van Dijk suggests that this is a common feature of elite racist discourse. Since it would be too openly racist to denigrate the marginalized groups, elites often attack the anti-racist whites with impunity. He proposes that racist elites may see the African American anti-racism activists as beneath their (the elites) station, and that only the white anti-racists "need to be taken seriously" (p. 93). The above passage should not be taken as an uncritical endorsement by van Dijk of white reformers, who as he points out can sometimes have paternalistic attitudes.

A major device utilized by elites is that of Vox Populi in which they claim to be speaking for the common man. For example, Sir John Stokes, member of the English House of Lords, said during a debate on immigration:

The burden of receiving and coping with these newcomers in
our midst has fallen not on the intellectuals, Labour Members
of Parliament and others of that ilk but on the ordinary English
working-class people.   Surely they are entitled to have a voice
here. (p. 100)

Sir John manages to brand liberals as elitist while setting himself
and other anti-immigrant Members of Parliament up as the voices of
the working class.   Such rhetoric is often couched in an appeal to
"common sense" values.   This leads to van Dijk's major thesis that
"legitimization" for the elites' role in furthering racist attitudes can be
found in claims of "popular support while at the same time pre-
formulating the terms that help create the state of mind that gives rise to
such support in the first place" (p. 100).   Politicians are joined by
media, corporate and other elites in this endeavor.

In a 2006 study, Julie Macleavy utilizes critical discourse analysis
to examine the ways politicians use discourse to establish support for
policies that ultimately disadvantage the subjects of the legislation.   In
her work, she suggests that elites often attempt to co-opt the language
of the opposition by re-interpreting the original meaning, but still piggy
backing upon the capital that the terms have earned through previous
context.   Macleavy looked at the use of the term "social exclusion,"
which was a major concern of the U. K.'s leftist Labour Party in
response to the fallout from the economic restructuring by the
conservative Tory Party.   When the Labour Party morphed into New
Labour, and assumed power in the 1990s, they continued to benefit
from the cachet they inherited along with the phrase "social exclusion."
However, there began a slow process of change in the rhetoric that
conceptualized the conditions behind the term.   Here is an example of a
description of social exclusion by the old Labour Party:

Social exclusion refers to the multiple and changing factors
resulting in people being excluded from the normal exchanges,
practices and rights of modern society.   Poverty is one of the
most obvious factors, but social exclusion also refers to
inadequate rights in housing, education, health and access to
services. (p.89)

In this interpretation, the emphasis is upon naming the factors that facilitate the *process* of social exclusion, according to Macleavy. People are marginalized due to lack of access to services that the writers see as basic rights. Compare this passage to that of the more centrist New Labour's rhetoric, written after the party gained power:

> Social exclusion is a shorthand term for what can happen when people or areas suffer from a combination of linked problems such as unemployment, poor skills, low incomes, poor housing, high crime environments, bad health and family breakdown. (p. 90)

In this passage, there is a subtle change from the focus on process to one of *conditions*. Social exclusion is no longer the result of denial of rights to basic services. Instead, it is the condition that results from the problems listed. The marginalized, in the new way of thinking, are no longer denied access to these services, they just lack them for reasons that relate to factors largely endogenous to the community and not to society as a whole. In addition, in the New Labour way of seeing exclusion, the marginalized bear responsibility for their own fates through such factors as high crime, poor skills and family breakdown. The author states that these are not isolated rhetorical incidences, but are representative of a pattern of subtle attempts to gain support for policies that ultimately harm the out-groups:

> Within New Labour discourse…social exclusion is understood within wider frameworks of meaning such as the agenda of 'rights and responsibilities' in which individuals must assume liability for their own circumstances. (p. 90)

Macleavy sees this discourse as a means to promote the larger agenda of "rallying the growing-number of individuals excluded from waged employment (and by implication, society more generally through construing contribution to the economy as *the* [emphasis hers] form of participation in social life) with supply side labour market policy" (p. 92). She suggests this new vision does little to address the concerns of the marginalized because of its shifting attention away from the role of the state in addressing societal inequities.

Macleavy's analysis provides an example of a researcher's process of weaving a thread between the rhetoric and the policies and the ways these dynamics can serve to establish common sense consensus around policies that benefit the elites while continuing to maintain the marginalization of the excluded. In addition, her study indicates the utility of studying how discourse changes over time.

John Wilson (2001) agrees with the importance of looking at word usage not only within the specific spatial frame of reference, but also as temporal patterns. "It is not only the single occurrence of a term that is important but sets of collocational relationships, which in their turn produce and draw upon ideological schemas in confirming or reconfirming particular views of the world" (p. 406). However, unlike MacLeavy's study, the salient factor was the lack of change over time. An example he cites relates to political discourse in apartheid South Africa. Blacks were described as belonging to mobs, crowds, and factions. They were portrayed as representative of the entire race whenever there were reports of violence or lawlessness. On the other hand, Whites who committed similar acts were depicted as loners or extremists, thus making it clear that what they were doing was atypical for their race. A single excerpt from a debate or newspaper account may not point to this relationship. Careful reading of multiple transcripts, however, could reveal similar patterns of usage indicating an apparent attempt to establish a false myth of Blacks being inherently violent.

Teun van Dijk (1987) suggests that systemic inequalities are formulated and reproduced through the discourse of elites. He defines elites as "social (minority) groups that have various types of power and control, whether political, economics, social, cultural, or personal" (van Dijk, 1987 p. 367). These elites, through various means, regulate the lives of the marginalized groups when their authority is perceived as legitimate. Elites can take several forms including symbolic and sociocultural elites. Within the cultural elite group, the power is covertly persuasive. Even without overt political power, they exercise control over discourse. The symbolic elites exert a high degree of influence over marginalized groups via the ability to both create and recreate hierarchies, and also by providing legitimacy to state and corporate policy that is either hierarchy enhancing or egalitarian (van Dijk, 1993).

In addition, there are the sociopolitical elite, which are embedded in the state apparatus (politicians), and economic elite who are the captains of finance, such as the CEOs and managers (van Dijk, 1987). Of course, there can be crossover between these various groups.

In this study, I examine the discourse of U.S. Senate and House members as they debated the 1994 Omnibus Crime Bill, particularly the amendments introduced to cut off Pell Grant funding for prisoners. I also look at the re-entry debates regarding the 2007 Second Chance Act. These transcripts are part of the Congressional Record, which includes the statements made on the floor of the U.S. House and the U.S. Senate. In addition, the Record contains the Extensions of Remarks, which is text added at a later time at the member's request.

Grbich (2007) suggests that the first step in discourse analysis can be to unveil the context that gives rise to the talk and text. This can be accomplished by revealing "the historical development of the discourse over time and identify the players and the social, economic and political climate which fostered its development" (p. 149). The revealing is the task I have attempted earlier in this work, using an analysis of the causes, progression and consequences of current policy toward prisoner education. Nicola Woods (2006) calls this the "top down" approach to discourse which first seeks to identify overall expectations and assumptions about and by those participating in the discourse before proceeding to analysis of the text and talk.

In order to further the reader's ability to place my interpretations of the text within context, I aimed to make the text excerpts provided in this work reasonably extensive.

After identifying the data related to the Congressional Record, the information was coded into six broad thematic categories. These included punitive talk (tough on prisoners), prison system failure, blocked opportunities (talk suggesting the need for inmate education, training, job placement, etc.), social breakdown (moral panic, faith-based talk, prisoner deficits) and rhetorical devices (strategies used to elicit support, such as nationalism or vox populi). In addition, there was a miscellaneous category for themes of interest that did not fit into the above five, such as counter-hegemonic talk. The first four categories were suggested by Sasson (1995) in his work *Crime Talk*.

After establishing general categories, I engaged the discourse through reading the content in order to identify overriding themes and the key stakeholders and their positions. Then, I approached the text through what James Gee (2005) calls "thinking devices" that serve to help build a convergence of evidence for both the themes evident in the discourse; and the overall expectations and assumptions that arose from the initial policy analysis. Examples of these devices included: World Building - identifying which institutions are constructed or are reconstructed; Political Building - how issues of power, status, gender, race and other hierarchy maintaining constructs are cogent and Connection Building - looking at temporal/spatial dynamics of the ideas, i.e. relationships to ideas in the past, or to come, or currently held ideas in other places. During the next stage, I examined how the overriding themes are constructed and maintained on the micro level of the debate interactions through the use of rhetorical devices such as the previously described vox populi, paternalism, and nationalism. Finally, I attempted to weave the conclusions drawn from the text together with the assumptions from the policy analysis into a description of the role of discourse in creating myths that maintain social hierarchies.

CHAPTER 5

The Pell Grant Debates

1994 Crime Bill

On April 11, 1989, Senator Arlen Specter, then a Republican from Pennsylvania issued the following warning on the floor of the U.S. Senate:

> Not since the 1920's has such widespread violence plagued our city streets. This lawlessness revolves around the illegal drug trade, and increasingly involves our Nation's young people. Children as young as 10 and 11 use and deal drugs. Unless we take immediate and vigorous action, we run the risk of fostering a permanent urban underclass living outside the common values of our society. Mr. President, the escalating market for crack, a potent smokeable cocaine derivative, has transformed portions of our cities into battlegrounds where territory is violently secured and protected by both youth and adult gangs. Frequently, these gangs are organized along racial and ethnic lines, although preserving a cultural identification is less central to gang formation than it once was. Traffic in narcotics, the use of automatic and semiautomatic weapons, and indiscriminate violence, together represent a dire change in the motives behind gang organization. Names that have become all too familiar to residents of our urban areas, in particular, are Jamaican Posses, which operate mainly on the east coast; and Bloods and Crips, which are among the most violent of west coast gangs, made up mostly of black youth identified by rituals and

talismans. Hispanic gangs, Pacific Asian gangs, and older gangs such as Hell's Angels, are among others that vie for pieces of the very lucrative illegal drug trade. (1989, p. S3626)

The passage has all of the traits of a typical moral panic. There is an enunciation of a societal problem requiring immediate action. The problem has stated origins in urban areas, but has the potential of extending beyond those boundaries. As in most moral panics, youth figure prominently. The situation also represents an attack upon the moral fabric of the nation. Specter's speech has other attributes that would characterize much of the discourse over the next twenty years as it relates to crime, criminals, and prisoner education. One is the tendency to establish boundary markers between those who commit crimes and the rest of society. In the excerpt above, the Senator takes pains to emphasize the archaic nature of the violators by placing them in the context of Prohibition, invoking the specter of another prominent moral panic of the past century, 1920s gangsterism.

The use of the verb "plagued" serves to pathologize both the problem and its apparent instigators by implying that the solution requires medical efforts typically used when faced with an outbreak of a deadly plague. Standard measures to be taken include three steps: 1) identification of the pathogen. 2) isolation. 3) eradication of the offending entity. Specter takes the first step by establishing his credentials as an authority whose status as an official, with experience and/or education that provide him with the gravitas to make judgments. He states in another section of the speech that he previously served as district attorney of Philadelphia, thereby establishing his qualifications to categorize. The perpetrators turning "our cities into battlegrounds" were identified as youth and adult gangs, specifically "Jamaican Posses," "Bloods and Crips" and "Hispanic gangs, Pacific Asian gangs, and older gangs such as the Hell's Angels." The "pathogens" are identified and classified entirely as people of color with the exception of the white, working class Hell's Angels.

Once coded, the offending entities are then separated or isolated. In this passage the Senator accomplishes an immediate discursive separation through the device of negative-other presentation. Specter, white and elite, groups the perpetrators of violence into categories based upon ethnic and class status. This establishes positive-self presentation because whites are not mentioned (except as the demonic working class bikers). Doubtless elite whites have some culpability in the drug trade and its accompanying violence, either on the demand or the supply side, but they are not mentioned. Isolation techniques continue as the speaker characterizes the offenders as being distinguished by their "rituals and talismans;" terms that conjure in their most benign form, subjects of anthropological study or in its most offensive, "savages" who must be civilized (or eradicated). The process of quarantine is furthered through the description of the particularly virulent nature of this plague, that separates it even from the gang warfare of the past, for today's gangs are involved in "Traffic in narcotics, the use of automatic and semiautomatic weapons, and indiscriminant violence [that] together represent a dire change in the motive behind gang organization." It would not be an exaggeration to suggest that these same attributes could be attached to other gangs, including the Mafia and other white criminal syndicates. Yet Specter does not name them, possibly for two reasons. One reason is that it would blur the distinctions between the white law-abiding citizens, and the criminals. The other is that his call for urgent action is predicated on the supposition of the unprecedented nature of the crisis that threatens "the common values of our society."

Eradication of the gangs is to be achieved, according to Specter, through the imposition of severe penalties, including the use of mandatory sentences. In order to facilitate the State's ability to accommodate the influx of prisoners, the speaker suggests the federal government provide a massive support program that would include grants for prison construction. In addition, he recommends legislation that would allow 145 former military bases to be turned over to local governments so that they could be utilized to build prisons to warehouse inmates.

There are several reasons why I chose the passage by Specter to begin this analysis of congressional debate over prisoner education from the past twenty years. It illustrates the tendency of both proponents and opponents of education for prisoners to categorize prisoners as the *Other*, a category of beings separate from the human race. Also, while this passage is an example of extreme speech, Specter himself was not considered extreme.

Arlen Specter is representative of the "moderate" members of the U.S. Congress. According to the Congressional Quarterly (1993) he was "one of the more liberal Republicans in the Senate, particularly on social issues" (p. 1283). Specter later joined the Democratic Party. Germane to the focus of this study, Specter has been a consistent advocate for prisoner education and job training. However, his rhetoric illustrated above, is indicative of the dominant discourse of the 1990s moral panic in congressional debate of the treatment of criminals. This moral panic enveloped both conservatives and liberals.

Specter is not the first politician to utilize the fear of crime to boost an agenda through the creation of a moral panic. Nor was Richard Nixon, but Nixon has been credited with being the first major Presidential candidate whose victory at the polls was, in large part, due to his "law and order" campaign theme (Harris, 1993). In 1968, Nixon warned that drug use was devastating a generation of young people. He continued to ride the theme for the next four years. His appeal to rising concerns over drug use helped him in his re-election bid over George McGovern. When asked how successful anti-crime rhetoric was as a campaign tactic, Nixon advisor Egil Kugh replied that it was a "slam dunk" (cited in Gest, 2001 p. 110). According to the journal of the American Bar Association, "Politicians have used crime or 'law and order' in elections with devastating and divisive success in every election since" (Harris, 1993, p, 138). In the early 1980s, Ronald Reagan ran a campaign that centered on portraying President Jimmy Carter as being simultaneously soft on communism, Islamic terrorists and criminals. During the Reagan Administration the War on Crime opened up another major front: The War on Drugs.

As a cheaper, high potency form of cocaine, known as "crack" became available on the streets, the White House hammered on a theme of inner-city drug epidemics spilling over into mainstream (i.e. white) America. Nancy Reagan publicized a simplistic approach to fighting drug abuse. Emphasizing the phrase "Just Say No," the campaign was derided for portraying drug use as a matter of just making the wrong moral choices. No matter what effect the slogan had on actually reducing substance abuse it certainly did not harm the effort to paint the Reagan White House as actively engaged in an anti-drug campaign (Gest, 2001). Reagan had his allies in fomenting the moral panic over drugs, including many of the media outlets.

In a study by Reeves and Campbell (1994), the authors performed an extensive examination of network news broadcasts between 1980 and 1988. They discovered there were 528 news stories that focused solely on the subject of cocaine. Their analysis pointed out the striking degree in which "journalistic coverage of defining moments in the cocaine narrative corroborated the drug control establishment's self-interested promotion of drug hysteria" (p. 103). They go on to suggest that the coverage did much to establish a dominant narrative of white users as victims of a drug epidemic largely instigated and perpetuated by people of color.

Some of the media coverage was sensationalist to the extreme. A well-known example is the case of "Jimmy's World," a *Washington Post* article by Janet Cooke. The story revolved around a Black, eight-year-old boy who became a heroin addict with the help of his low-income mother and her boyfriend. The story appeared to establish a narrative of the low morality and self-destructive nature of the Black, inner-city family. The Post article was widely circulated, causing its own mini-moral panic involving other news outlets sending reporters out to find their own pre-teen addicts. Eventually the story won the author the 1981 Pulitzer Prize. However, a month after the prize was awarded, an investigative report by Associated Press writers revealed that Cooke had fabricated the entire story. She had to return the Pulitzer. In her defense, the writer claimed that her editors at the *Washington Post* placed a tremendous amount of pressure on her and other writers to produce "true stories" documenting the drug epidemic. In their analysis of the events surrounding the Post incident, Reinarman and Duskin (2006) suggest that:

> If the Post scandal has value, it inheres in the accidental glimpse it affords into the nominally hidden process by which media institutions force the untidy facts of social life through the sieve of dominant ideology … and thereby helps to forge a public prepared to swallow the next junkie stereotype and to enlist in the next drug war. (p. 342)

Media sensationalism and political demagoguery colluded to drive the public into a virtual panic over drugs as the decade progressed. In 1985 only about 4% of the nation perceived drug abuse as the country's number one problem. By 1989, the year of Arlen Specter's speech, the number was up to 64% (Goode & Ben-Yehuda, 1994). This points to another reason why I chose to highlight Specter's speech, for it was situated chronologically in the interstitial space between the War on Drugs and the next moral panic over violent crime. Shades of each concern are found within the senator's rhetoric as he rails against both drug use and "indiscriminant violence."

In the early 1990s, media stories of an "epidemic" of violence greatly increased (Chiricos, Eschholz & Gertz, 2006). In the same period of time, there was a presidential election in which the Democratic candidate, Bill Clinton, sought to seize the mantle of crime crusader away from his Republican opponent. By advocating tough-on-crime measures in order to reposition the New Democrats in the eyes of voters, Clinton managed to keep the issue on the campaign agenda (Hohenburg, 1997). Public concern over violence reached a feverish pitch, fueled in part by the media, including those widely considered "liberal." Around the time of the crime bill debate Walter Cronkite hosted a four hour documentary on crime, *Victory Over Violence*, which advocated, among other measures, "guaranteed incarceration of serious offenders" (Kondracke, 1994, p. 1). According to Gallup, by 1994, the year the Omnibus Crime Bill passed, violent crime had become American's most pressing concern (Gallup, 1994). In this climate the fate of Pell grants for prisoners had been sealed.

Moral panic permeated the debate over the 1994 Crime Bill which was massive legislation that covered many areas of criminal justice, including gun control, the rights of the accused, grants for hiring police officers, an expansion of the death penalty, mandatory sentencing, prison construction, and the denial of the Pell Grant for prisoners.

The congressional debates leading up to the passage of the 1994 Crime Bill should be understood within the context of the concurrent political situation. After serving two years in office, President Bill Clinton's Democratic majorities in the House and the Senate were facing midterm elections. Traditionally, the party in power loses seats during midterm. Compounding this potential problem for the Democrats was President Clinton's drop in popularity in the polls, apparently aggravated by his party's inability to pass a promised healthcare reform bill (Hohenburg, 1997 p.15).

Nipping at Clinton's heels was a newly energized Republican Party led by an insurgent Newt Gingrich, pushing a platform of radical reform that would later be known as the *Contract with America*. The Republican manifesto included, among other provisions, a call for increases in military spending, deregulation, and welfare reform. In addition, the platform "embodies the Republican approach to fighting crime: making punishments severe enough to deter criminals from committing crimes" (p.38) by calling for mandatory sentences, reduction of *habeas corpus* appeals and increased prison construction (Gillespie, 1994). During the years leading to the midterm election, the Republicans were running hard on their traditional platform strengths; chief among them was the tough-on-crime issue. Pushed by the Right, the Democratic Congress was acutely aware of the scrutiny they were under in their precarious position as the dominant party.

The pressure on the 103rd Congress was intensified by the presence of C-SPAN cameras in the congressional chambers. The Cable Satellite Public Affairs Network (C-SPAN) began broadcasting Congressional debates in 1979, but it was several years before cable television became *du jour* in American homes. By the 1990s, the decade of the debates over the Omnibus Crime Bill, most Americans had a window into the lives of their elected officials to Congress. Over 70 million households had C-SPAN access. Politicians were acutely aware of this new medium and its potential as a gateway to hegemony. In her comparison of congressional debates of the 1800s, 1930s and 1980s, Cheryl Chambers (2011) suggests that the presence of the electronic media may have changed the way discourse was presented. She noted a shift away from actual back and forth discussions toward the recitation of prepared speeches. In addition, she proposes C-SPAN may have caused the members to be "more vocal to garner more camera time and more aware of their audience" (p. 217). A young Newt Gingrich, whose eventual rise to the position of House Speaker has been attributed to his masterful use of the chamber's cameras, told a reporter: "Conflict equals exposure equals power" (Congressional Quarterly, 2008, p. 6). It is important to understand that the representatives were talking to more than just each other when they debated.

In the course of the 1994 Crime Bill's intense debates some congressmen noted the gaze of the cameras; including one whom acknowledged "the 1.5 million folks watching" the proceedings (Dornan, 1994, p.H2628). Independent observers suggest the presence of the media had an effect on the politicians' behavior. Columnist George Will (1994), in an editorial for the Washington Post stated that, in addition to concerns over the economic costs, "In withdrawing Pell grants from prisoners the Senate may have been grandstanding and chest-thumping" (p. S1276).

Whether from genuine outrage or calculated political maneuvering, the rhetoric over the perceived crime wave sweeping the nation rose to new heights during the debates, much of it suggesting a fundamental breakdown in society. Senator Joe Biden (D-DE), future Vice-President and one of the chief architects of the Crime Bill stated:

> It is what we lose every day because of violence in America--promise, security, trust, hope, opportunity, justice, liberty--the very foundations of all that we cherish in our private and our communal lives are threatened by violent crime. (1993, p. S15967)

In his plea for action, Biden appealed to just about every level of the human hierarchy of needs with the exception of food and shelter. Much more inflammatory, was the moral panic exhibited by Robert Dornan (R-CA):

> There is a Federal role when our society is degenerating, when our culture is literally melting down, when we live in a country where the whole world points at us and refers to our child pornography, our drive-by shootings, our gangs and carjackings, where people are pulled out of cars by teenagers and beaten sometimes to death. Our culture is melting down. (1994, p. H2026)

Dornan couches the crime debate within the context of a cultural war. In another excerpt he states that the blame for the societal meltdown should be placed on the shoulders of 1960s radicals:

> What I said in a 1-minute speech earlier on the day we began debating the crime bill this week, most historians consider a

generation 30 years. A generation ago was in the spring in 1964. As the Barry Goldwater campaign was ginning up, Nelson Rockefeller was making the rounds in my party. It was then that the Filthy Speech Movement, even got it down to an acronym, the FSM, the Filthy Speech Movement, at the mother of universities in the western United States, Cal Berkeley, that Filthy Speech Movement started. Participants screamed every vile Anglo-Saxon word at the top of their voice and over bullhorns on the campus. That was the beginning of the roaring 1960's. Actually the 1960's were half over. I think if you look at an 11-year period from the spring of 1964 to April 30 of 1975, when Vietnam collapsed, Saigon fell to the Communist invaders, the 11-year period was one of drug glorification. The glorifying homosexuality as equal to normal family life. It was the beginning of saying if it feels good, do it. We were told to make love, Free love, Easy love, Love with strangers, Love in orgies, Switch-hitting, Wife-swapping. What they got was an AIDS epidemic that has killed 140,000. Within 2 years, death from AIDS will be five times the death toll in combat in Vietnam. Yes, a lot of it was energized by the liberals, no-win, no-victory-allowed war in Vietnam. When that 11 years was up, we had a generation, the baby-boomer generation, that was spoiled with too many of this world's goods and too much misdirected love because their families came through the hell of the Depression and then World War II. That baby-boomer generation that is now in its prime, pulling all the levers of power in some places including parts of this Congress and soon the Supreme Court, certainly over at the White House with its overabundance of flower children. (1994, p. H2627)

Like Specter in the earlier passage, who deftly provided a link between the moral panics over today's crime and earlier panics during Prohibition, so also does Dornan as he attempts to weave a narrative between a litany of today's alleged ills and the moral panic that arose in the 1960s over youth astray. In his diatribe, Dornan suggests the crime wave is another instance of chickens coming home to roost for a generation of "spoiled" baby-boomers whose previous indulgences in permissiveness he claims resulted in the AIDs epidemic and the loss of the Vietnam War. Taken out of context, the Congressman's extreme example of negative-other presentation seems to point to a Congressman unhinged. However, it is doubtful he could be re-elected to Congress for eight terms without some degree of political savvy.

Dornan's California district is heavily involved in the military-industrial complex, with large defense and aerospace companies providing the "backbone of the local economy" (Congressional Quarterly, 1993, p.235). A jab at the peacenik liberals would probably play well with the folks back home. In addition, Dornan's district is home to a large population of Vietnamese immigrants, a constituency he may perceive as being receptive to rhetoric that is critical of the regime they left behind; and the generation of Americans who allegedly fermented the circumstances that gave impetus to Hanoi's rise to power.

As I analyze the Congressional debates over the Crime Bill with its provisions for prison construction and the elimination of prisoner Pell grants among other features, it is important to keep in mind the possibility for economic and political subtexts that are not readily apparent in the speech acts of the participants.

The "Othering" of Prisoners

In the U.S. House, the fight to deny Pell Grants to prisoners was led by Bart Gordon (D-TN). Gordon represented a district bordering Nashville that "embodies qualities of both the Old and New South" (Congressional Quarterly, 1993, p. 1424) with both rural and suburban areas. Gordon's voting record is moderately liberal with high ratings from the AFL-CIO's grading of votes on labor issues and low scores from the American Conservative Union. In the early 1990s, Gordon may have started feeling some of the pressure from the Republican electoral tide sweeping the South. In 1990 he easily won re-election with 67% of the vote compared with 29% for his Republican opponent. In 1992, the year before he pushed through legislation denying Pell Grants for prisoners, Gordon won election by a considerably narrower margin of 57 to 41%, his lowest spread ever. That year Gordon sought publicity for his most precious cause: educational fraud. According to the *Congressional Quarterly*, removing access to Pell Grants for "shoddy" trade schools became a mission for Gordon, one in which he gained a considerable amount of publicity. While in Congress, he personally went undercover as a prospective student in a sting operation involving vocational schools as part of an NBC News expose (Congressional Quarterly, 1993). Gordon's attempts to gain maximum exposure from his causes, combined with his increasingly precarious state as a Southern White Democrat, increase the possibility his embrace of anti-crime rhetoric was an attempt to re-position himself in the eyes of voters.

Gordon tried several legislative tactics to deny prisoner Pell Grants, including attaching amendments to education bills (ultimately deleted from the legislation). But it was in the supercharged arena of the debate surrounding the Omnibus Crime Bill that Gordon met with success. Gordon spelled out his case for his legislation on the House floor:

> Let me remind Members that every time that a prisoner gets a Pell grant that means a traditional student does not get a Pell grant. Not only do they not get it, but since prisoners have no income, they are first in line. So nobody else gets a Pell grant until all of the prisoners, with no income, get what they want. (1992, p. H1893)

Here the congressman attempts to push the inmate students to the margins of consideration for Pell grants by identifying inmate students solely within the term "prisoner," not inmate student or men or women. Thus he de-personalizes those in prison as compared to "traditional students." Gordon also attempts to drive a wedge between Us and Them by suggesting that grants toward prisoner students somehow result in denial of grants to those who are not inmates. Unlike some grants and scholarships, Pell Grants have never been competitive. In addition, Gordon deftly turns one aspect of prisoner existence that would seemingly draw a modicum of sympathy, the prisoner's poverty, into a seeming advantage. Their lack of income puts them "first in line." The illocutionary effect of this rhetorical device would be to view incarcerated student's lack of personal income as some kind of unfair advantage over free students. In the world being constructed by

Gordon, being sentenced to prison placed them in a position of privilege. This position is enforced through another passage:

> Let me just relate to Members a true story that happened to me. It was about 4 or 5 weeks ago. A policeman in my hometown of Murfreesboro was talking to me about trying to help his son get some financial aid to go to school. We all know that policeman (sic) are not overly paid, but he made too much money to be able to get in any kind of a Pell grant program. Let me tell Members, that policeman's son could not get a Pell grant. But if he arrested someone for breaking into your house tonight and put them in jail, then they could get a Pell grant. That just does not seem to make much sense. (1992, p. H1893)

The tale apparently involved a member of the police department who tells the congressman he needs financial help for his son to continue his education. There the "true story" ends. No elaboration. Did his son achieve the minimal grade requirements for entrance? What kind of school was he attempting to enter? Not all institutions offer Pell grants. Not all majors are Pell Grant eligible, so what was his? Was it continuing education? Gordon admits the officer made too much money for his son to be eligible for Pell grants, although "we all know that policeman (sic) are not overly paid." Compared to whom? This sets up a "common sense" understanding in which it is assumed that all officers are underpaid, no matter what their rank.

In Gordon's world, like everyone's, the blank spaces are filled with implied understandings that are informed by shared values. However, unlike most people, he has an inordinate amount of influence in creating these values given his status. In Gordon's world, prisoners, who are blessed with no possessions, are taking advantage of police officers. It is likely that street cops are underpaid, but the same may be said of most firemen, teachers and mechanics, all of whom the congressman may have spoken to and obtained "true stories." Yet, Gordon for some reason chose this particular tale. It is possible he chose the narrative of the policeman to further re-enforce the binary between Us and Them. What better way to further marginalize inmates than to set up a contrast with the upholder of societal virtue: the policeman.

Further, by associating himself with the victims of the alleged scam perpetrated by the prisoners, Gordon sets himself up as defending the shared or "common sense" values; thus establishing his and his fellow elites' hegemonic position as the *vox populi* or spokesman for the people. This would surely play well with the folks back home in Murfreesboro.

Like a cascading of dominos, Gordon's cohorts (from both political parties) appeared to key in to his strategy. When opponents to the Gordon amendment offered up substitute legislation to deny prisoner Pell Grants only if and when research indicated they did not reduce recidivism, Jack Fields (R-TX), rose in unequivocal opposition:

> Mr. Chairman, today we have the opportunity, once and for all, to make incarcerated prisoners ineligible to receive Pell grants--the grant program designed to help low- and middle-income students meet the costs of attending college. We can do that by voting for the Gordon-Holden-Fields amendment to the crime bill. Today, incarcerated prisoners are applying for, and obtaining Pell grants. Every dollar in Pell grant funds obtained by prisoners means that fewer law-abiding students who need help in meeting their college costs are eligible for that assistance. It also means that law-abiding students who meet eligibility criteria receive smaller annual grants than they might otherwise obtain. Mr. Speaker, the Federal Government spends up to $100 million a year on education and training programs specifically targeted at prisoners--and that's more than enough, as far as I'm concerned. This amendment mandates that incarcerated prisoners be ineligible to receive Pell grants. Now. Period. No more studies, no more delays. It is a straightforward, simple amendment. If you oppose Pell grants for prisoners, you should vote for the Gordon-Holden-Fields amendment. We do not need any more studies. We need more higher education funds for our constituents' sons and daughters who are struggling to pay for their children's college expenses. Our constituents already pay to feed, house, clothe and rehabilitate prisoners. Their sons and daughters shouldn't have to do without so that incarcerated prisoners can use Pell grant funds to go to college. (1994, p. H2545)

Using seemingly populist rhetoric, Fields attempts to set up a binary between the imprisoned and the free by implying prisoners are virtual freeloaders living off the largesse of the taxpayer. To emphasize their status, Fields states that they are not only prisoners, but "*incarcerated* prisoners," [emphasis added] four times in his diatribe. Those who deserve Pell Grants are "law-abiding," "students" and "son and daughters," although prisoners who receive grants fall into [at least] two of those categories. Fields, through his syntactic choices, drives a wedge between the students on the outside and those on the inside.

Chief sponsor of prisoner Pell Grants legislation in the Senate was Kay Bailey Hutchison (R-TX). At the time of the debates, she had just won a special election to replace Senator Lloyd Bentsen who had accepted a cabinet position in the Clinton Administration. In the special election she won against the Democratic candidate to the office by a decisive margin of 67% to 33%. Her support was widespread across Texas and included every region with the exception of the extremely low-income, largely Hispanic border counties. Hutchison is considered a "tried and true Texas conservative" who has "anti-regulatory and pro-entrepreneurial beliefs" (Congressional Quarterly, 1993, p. 1443). In her speech, she appears to take a cue from her Democratic counterpart in the House, Gordon, by hitting upon similar themes of pitting prisoner students against non-prisoner students:

> My amendment is aimed at stretching every possible dollar for those young people who stay out of trouble, study hard, and deserve a chance to further their education, fair to working Americans who pay their taxes and do without in order that their children will have advantages they never had: a better education, more opportunities, a better future. The American people are frustrated by a Federal Government and a Congress that cannot seem to get priorities straight. They are frustrated and angry by a Federal Government that sets rules that put convicts at the head of the line for college financial aid, crowding out law abiding citizens. (1993, p. S15748)

In this passage she isolates inmate students to the margins of humanity by constructing a counter punctual lexicon between, on the one hand, "students," "people," "children," "Americans" and "citizens" and on the other, "convicts." Prisoners receiving the Pell are people and students and most are American citizens, but the Senator chooses not to include them as such. Hutchison, like Gordon and Fields in the previous passages, attempts to set herself up as a defender of the "working Americans'" interests by positioning herself as the spokesperson of that ubiquitous police officer whose child can't qualify for a Pell grant:

> One police officer whose daughter couldn't quality for a Pell grant summed up his frustration when he said recently, `Maybe I should take my badge off and rob a store. (1993, p. S15748)

In this telling of the "true story," the child is a daughter, not a son. In addition, the father's frustration over not qualifying for the Pell grant has raised to the point that he is contemplating going over to the other side through a life of crime. The implication is that the unfairness of current prisoner Pell Grant policy threatens the basic values of the nation, as epitomized by the police officer's moral quandary of whether he should turn to crime to finance his child's education.

There is one point in the previous excerpt where Hutchison attempts to bridge the space between the inmate students and the students on the outside, but the gap is crossed only at a point of conflict as the prisoners and non-prisoners metaphorically jockey for position to obtain financial aid. In her narrative she describes inmate students as "convicts" who go "to the head of the line for financial aid, crowding out law-abiding citizens." This phrase "crowding out" conjures two images: one of a large mass of prisoners, in itself having the potential to raise anxiety in the listener. Crowding out is accomplished through physical touch. Hutchinson takes the scene further in another passage:

> The Department of Education apparently is aware that as many as 100,000 youngsters are being elbowed aside by those behind bars. (1993, p. S15586)

In this statement she clinches her argument with a rhetorical flourish as she invokes the image of "100,000 youngsters" who are being "elbowed aside" by the undeserving convicts, thus establishing the discursive link between education policy run amok and physical violence against its young victims.

The similarities of Gordon's, Fields and Hutchison's rhetorical devices, within their contributions to the debate over the legislation to limit Pell Grants, suggest the possibility of intentional use of the same rhetorical devices and/or myths. The "true story" of the police officer who could not afford to send his child to college managed to spread from the Democratic to the Republican side of the aisle and even from the U.S. House building to the Senate building. All evoke images of hordes of convicts pushing helpless youngsters aside in their apparent bloodlust for a college education. The repetitive use of these images, both temporally and spatially, undoubtedly had an effect on the undiscerning listener and viewer through the establishment of a "common sense" worldview of Pell Grant policy. In this view it is only fair that access be cut off because the effect would be to tip the scales of justice toward some semblance of balance, thus setting up a situation where everyone wins when Pell Grants are cut off for prisoners. In the words of Senator Hutchison:

> As I said at the outset, this is not fair. It is not fair to taxpayers. It is not fair to law-abiding citizens. It is not fair to the victims of crime. But we can set things right. We only need to make a choice. And for me, it is an easy choice. (1993, p. S15746)

Hutchison presents a functionalist argument for cutting off prisoner Pell Grants by framing it as a win-win situation. Fairness is the order of the day – for the law-abiding taxpayer and the crime victim by making the rational decision, the common sense "easy choice" to deny prisoners the Pell Grant.

Arguments for Pell Grants

Opponents of inmates receiving Pell Grants for college courses had tried for several years before 1994 to delete authorization. They were, as illustrated above, an ideologically disparate group. Prisoner Pell Grant supporters appeared to have more ideological cohesion while representing two factions within the Democratic Party: The Congressional Black Caucus and the White, Northeastern liberals, such as Senator Edward Kennedy (D-MA) and Senator Claiborne Pell (D-RI).

As previously related, the opposition to prisoner Pell Grants relied primarily on a tactic of negative-other presentation with an attempt to marginalize prisoners outside of "normal" Americans. There were a few attempts by Pell Grant supporters to counter this narrative through a similar construct. Claiborne Pell (D-RI), in Senate debate, cited an editorial from the Washington Post that was in support of Pell Grants for prisoners. In the course of the article was the following passage:

> America's wardens and parole officers know what few in the Senate and House are willing to acknowledge in the crime bill debate: The more education inmates receive while in prison, the less likely it is they will commit crimes on release. Recidivism rates, which range between 60 and 70 percent in most states, are cut by as much as 80 percent among men and women who completed high school or college courses while in prison. Education equals prevention. Diplomas are crime stoppers. As Congress finishes work on what is expected to be a $22 billion crime bill, no increased funding for education programs is in the legislation. It's the other way. The Senate backed an amendment--sponsored by Kay Bailey Hutchison (R-Texas), who is currently under felony indictment for political abuses--to deny prisoners college courses under Pell grants. (1994, p. S1275)

The felony indictment mentioned in this passage was apparently a reference to allegations made against Hutchison for breaking election law during her recent election in which she allegedly tampered with state records regarding her use of state resources for campaign purposes (Congressional Quarterly, 1993). By mentioning these charges against Hutchison, Senator Pell may have been attempting to de-center her categorization of lawbreakers as outside society. Senator Pell, by blurring the space between Hutchison and prisoners problematizes her argument. Dislocations such as this, which lay manifest within the "real" world of the courtroom, may have been helpful in countering

Hutchison's attempts to construct a marginalized group in the eyes and ears of both the fellow Senators and the gaze of C-SPAN's audience. However, other than the mention of Hutchison's legal difficulties through the voice of the Post editorial, neither Senator Pell nor any other of the prisoner grant-supporting Senators mention the indictment in their own voices. There are a couple of possible reasons for Senator Pell's circumferential manner of introducing Hutchison's legal status. One may lie within the lived culture of the United States Senate, the other within the life of Senator Claiborne Pell. I will examine both.

Historically, the social language of the Senate tends to be less partisan and more deliberative than in the House Chamber. In their study of congressional debate over welfare reform of the same time period as the Omnibus Crime Bill legislation, Mucciaroni and Quirk (2006) found that the Senators speak for much longer periods of time than in the House, and they appeared to display more "historical knowledge." The "Senate debate was also less partisan and ideological in tone, with virtually none of the mutual disparagement and distrust of the other side that was frequent in the House" (p. 91). This study indicates why there tended to be fewer of the rhetorical "bomb throwers" in the Senate than in the House. A Newt Gingrich would be less likely to advance in the "gentleman's chamber" of the Senate due to his violation of the existent social language.

Mucciaroni and Quirk suggest there are several structural reasons why the differences in rhetorical style exist between the House and the Senate chambers. One is the size of the bodies with 100 Senators and 435 House members. This has an effect on debate style. Senators have more time to make their case, allowing for reasoned, thought-out argument without having to resort to clipped sound bites. In addition, Senators are up for re-election every six years instead of two. As a result, their speech is colored less by appeals to constituents for re-election than the House. Senate members also represent, for the most part, larger populations, which tend to display greater ideological diversity. I would add to the researchers' conclusions by suggesting that the relative size of the Senate, as well as the increased term lengths, probably breed greater interaction on both spatial and temporal planes, as the legislators spend more time together in a smaller social body. This is likely to potentiate collegial relationships, even across boundaries of party and ideology. Finally, the presence of the filibuster, a mechanism not found in House rules, reduces partisanship because legislation that is utterly abhorrent to the other side can be waylaid. This increases the likelihood Senators will reach out to members of the opposing party to co-sponsor legislation. For these reasons, personal attacks tend to be rare in Senate debate. So why did Senator Pell, a Senator described as "unfailingly gracious," break the chamber's social rules by drawing attention to Hutchison's felony indictment? Reasons may be found in the passion Senator Pell felt toward maintaining the Pell Grant's founding mission: To help society's most marginalized members gain access to college education. This was a mission that he played a key role in originating.

Senator Claiborne Pell came from a long line of wealthy power brokers, including his father who was a member of Congress. The Princeton-educated Pell took an early interest in helping the oppressed. In 1940, at the age of 22, he was one of the few U.S. non-Jews at the time who tried to help Jews in German-occupied Europe. He was twice arrested by the Nazis while trying to free concentration camp inmates. Pell was first elected to the U.S. Senate in 1960. By 1993 he was one of the most senior members, having been re-elected six times. Highly popular in his home state, he rarely received less than 60 % of the vote in an election. Having received a score averaging in the 90s by the AFL-CIO rating system and in the 20s from the U.S. Chamber of Commerce, his popularity in his New England home state may have been buttressed by Senator Pell's liberal voting record. His stature in the Senate was elevated by his position as chair of the Foreign Relations Committee where he was a staunch opponent of Ronald Reagan's intervention in Central America (Congressional Quarterly, 1993). He also took the lead role in drafting legislation to create the National Endowment for the Arts and the Amtrak railway system. However, it was his efforts in the area of equal access to college education that the Senator gained his lasting claim to fame.

In his first few years in office, Senator Pell quickly became one of the primary advocates for equal opportunity in higher education by initiating a comprehensive study on the issue. In part due to the findings, legislation was passed establishing the Basic Educational Opportunity Grant (BEOG), the means-based program for providing financial aid for low-income college students. In the years since, Senator Pell was a tireless opponent of efforts to water down the program. Tens of millions of students have received support from BEOG. In the 1980s, in recognition of his efforts, the Senate re-designated the program as the Pell Grant. The Senator was later asked how exactly the name change came about and the always jovial legislator replied that it was "because there was no Senator Beog!" (Honan, January 2, 2009).

It was possible that Senator Pell took the socially risky step of calling Hutchison out in denying Pell Grants to felons, saying she was under felony indictment because he saw funding denial as another assault on a program he had carefully nurtured for over 30 years. Attempts were made to whittle down funding by narrowing income requirements for all students. In the couple of years before this debate, felons who had served time were restricted from Pell Grant access. The year before, in a compromise with prisoner Pell Grant opponents, inmate students who were either on death row or serving life sentences were denied access. Senator Pell, perhaps sensing that his program was suffering a "death by a thousand cuts," took the uncharacteristic step of challenging Hutchison on a personal level.

There was one other attempt to de-center the prisoner Pell Grant opponents' attempts to marginalize prisoner students:

> Mr. President, I particularly want to clarify what may be some misunderstanding about the participation of the incarcerated in the Pell grant program. It is important to understand, at the outset, that no prisoner displaces another deserving student who is not in prison. The Pell grant program functions as a quasi-entitlement in which a student qualifies for a grant, and the size of the grant depends on the availability of sufficient appropriations. Thus, a student is not cut out of the program because a prisoner qualifies for a grant. If they are both eligible, they both receive a grant and there is little relationship between the two. (1993, p. S15967)

Senator Pell, who probably knew more about the Pell Grant program than anyone in the chamber, uses his status to make an authoritative argument to provide a counter thrust to his opponents' suppositions. In the passage above, Senator Pell is back to his gracious, patrician persona. He does not claim that the opposition deliberately lied in their statements that prisoner students deny Pell Grants to other students, but rather there "may be some misunderstanding." In addition, the Senator counters Hutchison's hegemonic rhetoric in several subtle ways. He states that "no prisoner displaces another deserving student." The implication is the prisoners also deserve grants. There is some aspect of that group that qualifies them as grantees. The listener is left to fill in the space: Is it income status? This indeed would be a radical notion since the prevailing descriptor of choice for income level is "qualifying" for grants not "deserving." The Senator may have intended to imply that the prisoner students deserve financial aid due to their willingness to obtain an education based upon completion of college prerequisites such as a high school diploma or GED. Since over a third of incarcerated individuals have not successfully completed that step, it certainly is not a given. Senator Pell may also be implying that prisoner students deserve the grant based on their status as a member of humanity, a position not out of character for a man who spent his life working in the interests of those being pushed to the margins, whether they were concentration camp inmates in the 1940s Europe, urban Blacks in the 1960s, campesinos in the 1980s Central America or America's prisoners in the time of this debate. They all appear to have been deserving in his worldview.

On a policy level, his authority comes into play as he carefully explains that the Pell Grant program is a "quasi-entitlement" in that all students who qualify are able to receive funding, the only variable being the amount appropriated for that year by Congress. The non-prisoner student and the inmate student both are eligible. Again, this was a very effective counter-thrust by the Senator. By using the social language of the culture "entitlement," the Senator is stating, in the jargon of the state, that Pell grants are available to all those applicants who are "entitled" or, in other words, deserve the grants, whether inside the prison system or not. Secondly, he qualifies the term entitlement, with the prefix quasi. Again, a descriptor that would have specific connotations within the chamber, yet the commonplace use of the morpheme does little to blunt its impact as a means to problematize the root. In this instance, the boundaries are blurred between what is an entitlement and what is not. One question that arises is how the boundaries are blurred since Senator Pell, in context, clearly prefers that the program be considered and operationally act as an entitlement. He provides clues in the next part of the sentence: "and the size of the grant depends on the availability of sufficient appropriations." The Senate has to vote every year on the funding levels for the highly popular program. The statement may have been intended as a verbal jab at the opposition Republicans, who, as a rule oppose extending Pell Grant status to that of an entitlement with full funding being guaranteed year by year. In the House, where Republicans tend to be more ideological, they have no problem admitting to the dichotomy of claiming to defend the non-prisoner students' rights to a share of Pell Grants while simultaneously resisting elevating the program to entitlement status. Here is a statement by Representative Steve Gunderson (R-WI):

> Mr. Chairman, we are not only opposed to Pell Grants being an entitlement. I hope we are also opposed to prisoners receiving priority over half the students in this country who are entitled to Pell grants and do not receive them. (1992, p. H1896)

Additionally, House Democrats appear to have no problem overtly calling prisoner Pell opponents on their hypocrisy as indicated by this statement from Representative Major Owens (D-NY):

> To my colleagues who are so concerned that there are not enough Pell grants to give one to every student who is eligible, I ask them to defend their decision to oppose the Pell grant entitlement that was originally included in H.R. 3553. Where was their concern for these students when they objected to the Pell grant entitlement? Pell grants for prisoners is a tiny drop in the bucket of student aid funds--but it is a very important drop. (1992, p. H1896)

In the rarified air of the Senate, such overt accusations of hypocrisy would not only violate the social language, it would also go against Senator Pell's demeanor. However, in the instance of calling Senator Hutchison out on her felony indictment through the vehicle of the newspaper editorial, he does not appear to be above allowing the illocutionary force of his speech act to accomplish the same goal when his life's work is threatened.

In furthering his arguments, the Senator counters the opposition's numbers argument:

> Also, regarding the number of prisoners who receive Pell grants, the Inspector General at the U.S. Department of Education estimates that the number is far less than the 100,000 figure that has been cited, and is actually only about 25,000. This is less than one-half of 1 percent of the 4.5 million students who received Pell grants last year. Further, the actual cost is also considerably less than the $200 million cited, and is much closer to $40 million, which is about six-tenths of 1 percent of the total Pell appropriation. (1993, p. S15967)

Here he enhances his position as an authority by citing specific sources for his data, unlike Hutchison and her House counterpart, Gordon who do not cite sources. At the time of these debates, the U.S. Department of Education stated that of the total of 5.3 billion awarded for Pell Grants for the 1993-1994 academic year, 35 million went to the women and men who were incarcerated. Only 27,000 prisoners received Pell Grants out of the 3.3 million total recipients (Zook, 1994). Pell further extends his economic argument:

> Mr. President, today there are currently more than 1,000,000 men and women in our Nation's jails. The cost of incarceration of this magnitude is enormous. On average, we spend $30,000 a year to keep a person in jail. As I have said on many, many occasions, it costs us more to send a person to jail than to Yale. Education is our primary hope for rehabilitating prisoners. Without education, I am afraid we are doomed to a recidivism rate of somewhere between 50 and 70 percent. The door into jail will remain a revolving one. With little or no education, a person will leave prison only to commit another crime and be returned to prison. (1993, S15967)

The Senator deftly weaves several points. First he states the magnitude of the problem by citing the incarceration rate of the time. Next, he attempts to de-center the opposition's Us and Them argument by positioning prisoners as "men and women," a recognition of humanity not afforded by those on the other side of the issue (or even by some on Senator Pell's side). He then provides his admittedly oft used sound bite "it costs us more to send a person to jail than to Yale." Using Yale not only satisfies the phrase's rhyming scheme, it also lifts prisoners into the class of the students both capable and deserving of attending the most elite Ivy League schools. Thus, he establishes a counter-hegemonic understanding of the irrationality of denial of Pell grant funding. He uses his position as an authority figure to issue the dire prediction that the proposed changes are "doomed" to failure as those inadequately educated are released and return to a life of criminal activity. In his narrative, the good Senator makes a prediction that would sadly come true over the next decade with the spike in incarceration rates.

Congressional Black Caucus

The Congressional Black Caucus took a leading position in opposing the elimination of Pell Grants for incarcerated students. A caucus, in the parlance of the U.S. Congress, can indicate the official role of a specific political party, as in the Republican Party Caucus or Democratic Party Caucus; or it can apply to an unofficial body of representatives who are ideologically like-minded or have similar interests. Examples of informal caucuses include the Hispanic Caucus, the Blue Dog Caucus (conservative Democrats), the Children's Caucus and the Congressional Black Caucus (Kravitz, 1993).

The Congressional Black Caucus was founded in 1971. At the time it was primarily concerned with power sharing in the U.S. House. The original thirteen members, some of whom were newly elected in the aftermath of major civil rights gains of the 1960s, found that once they had gained access to the halls of power they were being shut out of important committee assignments by the official caucuses, primarily the Democratic Caucus, the party of most Black Caucus members. Committees, by the rules of the legislative branch, are where most of the bills live or die, thus the Black representatives, to a large degree, were still denied a major role in the legislative process. Organizing itself largely along the lines of a labor union, with an emphasis on ideological solidarity, the Black Caucus is considered progressive. According to the Congressional Black Caucus newsletter (2011):

> Since 1971, the Members of the Congressional Black Caucus have joined together to strengthen their efforts to empower America's neglected citizens - including but not limited to Americans of color - by more effectively addressing our legislative concerns. (p. 2)

The Congressional Black Caucus tends to support state solutions to most societal ills; including increased welfare funding, financial aid enhancement, and budget shifts from the military to social programs and advances in civil rights legislation. The U.S. Chamber of Commerce, in its ratings of pro-free enterprise votes of members of Congress, calculated that Congressional Black Caucus members sided with the Chamber of Commerce position 15.6 % of the time compared with 33.6 % of the time for the Democratic Caucus as a whole. The reputation Congressional Black Caucus members had for "radical positions" undoubtedly sprang from both its voting record and from many caucus members' roots in 1960s protests. Members have included Martin Luther King cohorts Andrew Young and John Lewis, as well as former Black Panther Bobby Rush and anti-war activist Ron Dellums. These associations historically made it difficult to obtain seats on some very powerful, but ideologically conservative committees such as the Armed Services Committee (Singh, 1998).

In addition to a tendency toward shared political values, the Congressional Black Caucus, at least in its early years, relied a great deal on collective action in order to breach the rigid committee system in the U.S. House. An example is found in the attempt by Ron Dellums (D-CA) to obtain a seat on the Armed Services Committee. One of the most influential committees in Congress, Armed Services had a wide ranging scope of responsibilities in regards to defense; from military appropriations and defense contracts, to oversight of military intervention abroad and operations of the Central Intelligence Agency. Ron Dellums, whose district included Berkeley, California, was an avid opponent of military intervention. While a member of Congress, he had been beaten while participating in an anti-Vietnam War protest. His attempt to gain a seat on the Armed Services Committee was rebuffed by the Democratic Caucus leaders, who informed the Black Caucus that they would be willing to seat a Black member on the Armed Services Committee, but not the pacifist Dellums. The chair of the Black Caucus, Louis Stokes, told the Democratic leaders that "this is 1974 and in 1974, white people don't tell black people who their leaders are" (Singh, 1998, p. 79). Dellums was eventually seated.

Congressional committees slowly opened themselves up to Black representation. However, just as the Congressional Black Caucus gained members and power, its mission became slightly less focused as a new generation of Black Congresspersons gained office who were somewhat more ideologically diverse. Holding office for the first time in 1993 were moderate members of the Black Caucus, including several from the South (Singh, 1998). For the most part however, the Black Caucus supported Pell Grants for prisoners and some of its members led the debates to preserve them. They included Major Owens (D-NY), Ed Towns (D-NY), John Conyers (D-MI), and Albert Wynn (D-MD).

When debating the issue of Pell Grants for prisoners, members of the Black Caucus tended to utilize arguments centered around economics and recidivism. John Conyers (D-MI) who was a prominent Black Caucus member during the time of the Pell grant debates offered the following statement of record:

> Surprisingly, the amount of Pell grants used by the incarcerated is limited, often estimated to be less than 1.08 percent of Pell appropriations for last year. Statistics clearly show that this meager investment will radically improve an inmate's chances of permanent rehabilitation. According to the Department of Justice, recidivism rates for inmates participating in college programs was reduced from over 30 percent to a mere 11 percent. This means that 19 percent of those individuals who would have otherwise used taxpayers' money through trials and imprisonment, were instead contributing to society by working and paying their share of taxes. Most importantly, when you consider that it costs $30,000 per year to keep an individual in prison, this means a

> savings of $570,000 for every 100 inmates who do not return
> to crime. (1992, p. H1895)

Here, Conyers offers a data-backed examination of the benefits of prisoner education. He advocates for both the inmates and the tax paying non-prisoners. In laying out his reasons for supporting Pell Grants for students in prison, Conyers narrows the argument down to a business-like proposition involving an "investment" resulting in "savings" above "costs."

Ed Towns (D-NY), who served as Black Caucus chair from 1991 to 1992, followed a similar line. Here is a statement supporting a colleague's substitute amendment meant to forestall Gordon's Pell Grant elimination by restricting prisoner access to the Pell only if the Education Secretary certifies that the Pell doesn't reduce recidivism:

> This amendment uses a very simple cost benefit analysis to
> determine whether Pell grants should be eliminated by 1996.
> It must be clearly demonstrated on a Federal and State level
> that the benefits derived from inmates' utilization of Pell
> grants outweigh the costs associated with the program. I
> firmly believe that our prison system should utilize not only
> punitive, but rehabilitative measures that will enable inmates
> to become contributing members of society. Pell grants are a
> vital tool that can assist inmates in developing intellectually,
> and socially. Pell grants for inmates make sense and pay
> dividends in the short and long run. (1994, p. H2547)

Rep. Towns also takes a standpoint using the language of commerce: "cost-benefit analysis," and "benefits...outweigh...costs." The argument puts the position of the government into that of an investment firm, for whom capital outlay is justified primarily in terms of paying "dividends" rhetorically defined in monetary terms.

Kweisi Mfume (D-MD) succeeded Towns as a chairperson of the Black Caucus. In his statement in favor of prisoner Pell grants he decried the legislation for its inability to prepare prisoners for their post-release as "productive members of society."

At a cost of over $30,000 a year to keep someone behind bars, it is more expensive to send someone to prison than to Yale. In addition, recidivism rates that average 50-70 percent can be reduced to 15-30 percent through post-secondary education while incarcerated. It is very unfortunate that this crime bill does not give offenders the chance to turn their life around through education and become productive members of society upon their release. (1994, p. H9000)

Although Mfume offers the incarcerated student the opportunity to re-enter society it is under the stipulation that he be "productive." He suggests that the purpose of Pell Grants, at least in terms of prisoners, is to create a citizen who can "produce" for society. Representative Conyers made a similar statement two years prior.

Why should the American taxpayer reward incarcerated individuals with the privilege of education when the pool of funding is depleting rapidly for the rest of society? The answer is simple and well documented: By providing the tools of learning and self-improvement, society can reap the benefits of creative, productive citizens, as well as break the cycle of crime and prison. (1992, p. H1895)

Representative Conyers again suggests a cost-benefit analysis with the taxpayers serving as investors. Then he describes the ultimate dividend that society will "reap" by "providing the tools of learning and self-improvement." The profit would come in the form of a prisoner made into a new entity, a "productive" citizen. In a later passage from the same speech, he further defines the parameters of this reconstructed person and the ultimate goal of the improved self:

It's obvious that the most practical rehabilitative tool is education. Education socializes and provides a positive self-image which lasts an individual long after his sentence has been completed and well into his role as a hard-working, contributing member of society. I urge you to defeate [sic] this amendment. (1992, p. H1895)

Education is conceptualized as a tool and the product of that tool is a "positive self-image" of the "role as a hard-working, contributing" citizen. The newly-made self is defined, as previously described within a construct of economics. Thus, the goal of education is to create self-awareness as a rehabilitated being. To engender human capital for the labor market, both in mind and body. To create what Colin Gordon (1991) refers to as an *economic man*. As noted earlier, the ideal Western man must above all else be economically productive.

Members of the Black Caucus were not alone in their reconstruction of the educated prisoner along the strictures of commerce. Bill Goodling (R-PA), reliably conservative on most issues, was one of the few Republicans who supported prisoner Pell grants. His stand may have arisen, in part, from his background as a high school principal before his election to Congress. His arguments appeared to mirror those cited above.

> When we think that it costs $30,000 per year to reincarcerate someone or to send them to prison in the first place, that is a big bite for the taxpayer to pay. If, they are not on death row and they are not there for life, it seems to me what we should be trying to do is bring them back into society as well educated as we possibly can so that as a matter of fact they have an opportunity to get a job and be productive citizens and not cost the taxpayers $30,000 a year. (1992, p. H1893)

Once again, a college education is imagined as a tool to mold the inmate student into the ideal citizen "brought back into society" as if prison were an aberration (and by extension so are prisoners) that is not part of the social milieu. Education is seen solely as a means "to get a job" so the ideal citizen will not be a burden on the taxpayers.

In the ten years following the passage of the 1994 Crime Bill, with its harsh penalties and massive prison construction America's incarceration rates skyrocketed (Ruddell, 2004). Ever increasing numbers of former inmates began reentering communities with little support and they often returned to crime. This revolving door placed financial burdens on the criminal justice system. The conditions set the stage for the next major federal crime control legislation a decade after the enactment of the 1994 legislation: The Second Chance Act.

CHAPTER 6

The Second Chance Act Debates

At the beginning of 2004 an extraordinary speech was given in the U.S. House chamber. Here is an excerpt:

> Tonight I ask you to consider another group of Americans in need of help. This year, some 600,000 inmates will be released from prison back into society. We know from long experience that if they can't find work, or a home, or help, they are much more likely to commit crime and return to prison. So tonight, I propose a four-year, $300 million prisoner re-entry initiative to expand job training and placement services, to provide transitional housing, and to help newly released prisoners get mentoring, including from faith-based groups. America is the land of second chance, and when the gates of the prison open, the path ahead should lead to a better life. (State of the Union Address, 2004, p. 2)

What made this speech so startling was not the content, for others had called for major initiatives to help prisoners transition back into society. What was unusual was who was speaking, for it was one of the most conservative presidents in American history - George W. Bush. President Bush did not originate the war on crime. He was, however, one of the leading advocates. Going back to his time as Texas governor, Bush spent much of his political career advancing tough measures such as the expansion of the death penalty, mandatory sentencing and building more prisons (Perkinson, 2010). He was equally dedicated to cutting social programs. In the same address that he used to promote the prisoner program, Bush laid out a vision for a federal budget that would "limit the burden of government on the economy" through privatization of Social Security and other proposals to reduce the size of the state.

When Representative Danny Davis (D-IL), who was in the audience, heard the President suggest the creation of this massive federal program for prisoners, he said he "almost jumped out of my seat," so great was his shock (Second Chance Hearing, 2005, p. 13). Undoubtedly, Davis' surprise was shared by many of the representatives in the chamber who were so used to the White House opposing even relatively popular social programs like children's healthcare and Head Start. Such initiatives are designed to give the most vulnerable their first chance in life. So why was the President now proposing a massive government program that, in his words, gave convicted felons a "second chance?"

By the time of Bush's address many of the war on crime's most ardent supporters had realized that the explosion in America's prison population was not sustainable. In 2004 the number of men, women and children who were incarcerated was close to 2 million. Those in Congress who led the fight for harsh sentencing guidelines and a buildup of the prison system the previous decade began to see the impact of their push to incarcerate. Senator Joseph Biden (D-DE) was one of the chief sponsors of the 1994 legislation, calling it "my 1994 Crime Bill" and was a strong advocate of the harsh crime control measures that precipitated the massive growth in prison rates. Ten years after the passage of that bill, he engages in a little introspection regarding his actions:

> All too often we think about today, but not tomorrow. We look to short-term solutions for long- term problems. We need to have a change in thinking and approach. It's time we face the dire situation of prisoners reentering our communities with insufficient monitoring, little or no job skills, inadequate drug treatment, insufficient housing, lack of positive influences, a paucity of basic physical and mental health services, and deficient basic life skills. (2004, p. S10717)

In another passage, Biden describes the consequence of not acting.

> These huge numbers of released prisoners each year and the out-of-control recidivism rates are a recipe for disaster-- leading to untold damage, hardship, and death for victims; ruined futures and lost potential for re-offenders; and a huge drain on society at large. One particularly vulnerable group is the children of these offenders. We simply cannot be resigned to allowing generation after generation entering and reentering our prisons. This pernicious cycle must come to an end. (2004, p. S10717)

Whereas in 1994 the moral panic was over crime, here the Senator broadens the narrative's focus to include the impact on the prisoners, the victims, and for the first time, the children of the prisoners. Yet the emphasis is not on the suffering the prisoner's children will experience, for that is not mentioned, but on the "disaster leading to untold damage, hardship and death for victims." The only descriptor of impact on children is that they will become part of "generation after generation entering and reentering our prisons." In another passage from the same speech he spells out the impact of this high recidivism:

> Here's the kicker--a staggering 2/3 of these released state prisoners are expected to be rearrested for a felony or serious misdemeanor within 3 years of release. Two out of every three! You're talking about hundreds of thousands of reoffending ex-offenders each year and hundreds of thousands of serious crimes being committed by people who have already served time in jail. (2004, p. S10717)

The Senator's primary concern, "the kicker," is the effect of these released prisoners - and by extension, their children - will have on crime rates. Although in the introductory passage Senator Biden engages in a bit of reflection, the re-examination appears to be one that involves strategy and not goals. The men, women, and children who are prisoners or potential prisoners are valued only in terms of their ability or inability to commit crimes or become a "huge drain on society." There seems to be no change in the perception of prisoners as the Other, only on what strategy would best serve to go about "monitoring" them.

The potential of recidivist crime was not the only impetus for giving the men and women behind bars a second chance. The expansion of the penal system since the early 1990s began to create strains on government budgets. In his speech, President Bush acknowledged this fact commenting that the "high recidivism rate places a huge financial burden on taxpayers." Bush was not alone in having this view. Most U.S. prisons are constructed and maintained at the state level. A decade after the 1994 crime bill provided grants and other financial incentives for prison building, the states were starting to feel a budgetary pinch. The states were stuck paying the tab for the staffing, facility management, and prisoner needs, including medical care. This has been estimated to cost at least $30,000 per prisoner each year (Greenhouse, 2011). According to the Associated Press (2009): "Tough sentencing laws passed in the crime-busting 1980s and 1990s are largely to blame. Its fueling an explosion in inmate health costs for cash-strapped states" (p.1). The War on Crime precipitated ever increasing numbers of prisoners. With many three time offenders serving mandatory life sentences, the prison population was getting older, leading to higher health costs. A gathering of centrist governors issued a warning that: "a dramatic rise in the number of prisoners coming home over the next few years… threatens to engulf the United States" (ABC News, 2008 p.1). Compounding the financial burden to the states was the federal regulation denying inmates Medicaid or Medicare. According to McCaffery (2007), the southern states, which generally had the harshest crime policies, were hit particularly hard by the financial burdens, "in 16 southern states, the growth rate has escalated by an average of 145% since 1997" (p.1). Perhaps germane to President Bush's sudden embrace of prison reform was the fact that southern states provided the bulk of his and the Republican Party's support.

The governors of these states recognized the situation they were in and some have become actively involved in lobbying Congress for help. Maryland Governor Robert Erlrich, a Republican, testified before a congressional hearing in support of the Second Chance Act (Second Chance Hearing, p. 2005). Even the "wealthy" states were feeling the pinch. In states where the budgets were suffering, governors did not wait for the Second Chance Act to take effect before taking action. In Kentucky, the prison population was "soaring," and the state released 2000 inmates in a "temporary cost saving program." California's Republican governor Arnold Schwarzenegger attempted to reduce the number of state prisoners by releasing them early due to budgetary problems (Associated Press, 2009). Joan Petersillia (2011), who worked in the California governor's corrections office described the situation:

> [California] pours 10 percent of its massive state budget into correctional facilities. Between 1985 and 2005, it built 21 new prisons--more than one a year. The state's prison population surged, and so did costs: The state spent nearly $10 billion on corrections last year, or about $50,000 per prisoner (the national average is $23,000). Now that California is grappling with a budget crisis, it is clear that it cannot continue on this course. The evidence for the rest of the country may be less dramatic, but it is no less clear. (p.51)

For the governors who had made political careers of being tough on criminals, the newfound leniency was probably not the result of a change of heart regarding the plight of the men, women, and children who are imprisoned, but from the cold, budget-related calculations. The general support that surrounded the punitive strategies on crime control was starting to unravel under harsh economic realities.

A rise in the numbers of inmates led to an increase in those cycling back out of prisons. They faced many roadblocks preventing them from becoming financially self-supporting. These barriers included criminal records, gaps in their employment histories, as well as a job market where application procedures had changed. Applying for many positions now required a degree of computer literacy (Stern, 2006). In addition, the increase in industrialization, outsourcing and an increase in flexibilization greatly reduced the numbers of available good paying jobs with benefits (Wacquant, 1999).

Compounding the re-entry problem for former prisoners was an increase in information sharing that provided employers with greater access to criminal justice databases. Consequently, jobs that may have one time been easily available to ex-inmates now require criminal background checks. In their zeal to punish those who committed crimes, the lawmakers increased the sanctions against ex-prisoners using government social programs. Ex-felons were banned from living in public housing and had their drivers' licenses suspended (Stern, 2006). In addition, they may be barred from receiving student aid or welfare. The very assistance that could help the women and men return to their families and larger community had been cut off. Even their rights as parents were restricted. In his testimony in a 2005 Congressional Hearing on prisoner re-entry, Representative Danny Davis (D-IL) called these the "invisible punishments" of prisoners (Second Chance Hearing, p. 2005, p. 61).

With the full effect of the War on Crime and massive incarceration now rippling throughout society - from the communities to the state budgets all the way up to the White House - it is not surprising that a move to set up a federal program to reduce recidivism would gain support across the political spectrum. The kinds of organizations that came out in favor of the Second Chance Act reflect this ideological diversity. Generally liberal groups included the American Bar Association, the Children's Defense Fund, the NAACP and the National Council of La Raza. More conservative endorsers were the American Conservative Union, the Christian Coalition, the Family Research Council and the National Sheriff's Association (Brownback, 2008, p. S2938). Given the broad range of organizations supporting prisoner re-entry efforts, as well as pressure from the governors and the then-popular President, it is not surprising that Congress swung into action.

Second Chance Act Opponents

<u>Us and Them</u>
Despite the bi-partisan nature of the Second Chance Act supporters, the legislation still had its detractors. Among them was Representative Louie Gohmert (R-TX), who attempted to set up a competition for federal dollars between those who are incarcerated and those who are not:

> Like so many things that have been done in this body that has unintended consequences, the Second Chance Act is very

well intentioned. As a former judge, I know well that we have got to do a better job of rehabilitating, of educating, with drug treatment and alcohol treatment for those that are incarcerated in our prisons. There is just no question that we should do a better job with those things. Unfortunately, this well-meaning bill, the Second Chance Act, goes so far beyond what is helpful. (2007, p. H5283)

In this passage Gohmert utilizes the rhetorical device of "tough, but fair" by conceding the need for re-entry programs. However, he states his opposition to the specifics of the Act as an authority, a judge who supports prisoner education and rehabilitation, but not in context of the Second Chance Act. He makes the claim that the bill's provisions providing small grants to states to subsidize prisoner healthcare have the potential to grow into a massive federal program:

For example, this bill apparently will provide over $360 million. I say apparently will provide over that amount, because one provision says ``such sums as may be necessary." There is no way to know how much money that may be. But, in any event, this bill, for example, seems to leave medical care potentially unending after confinement. (2007, p. 5283)

He goes on to draw attention to the Second Chance Act's provisions that would help to rectify the problem of prisoners being isolated from their families by providing small demonstration grants to some states to help families with transportation, to and from prisons for visitation. Here, Gohmert tries to depict this funding as a denial to servicemen and women.

When a military member is sent to serve on one of the many unaccompanied tours of duty, his family suffers greatly, particularly if this is a Reservist or a National Guard member. However, under this Second Chance Act, which is really more of an ``Infinite Chance Act," we will provide taxpayer dollars to help with transportation for an inmate's family to get to and from the prison. Grant dollars are there for that. (2007, p. H5283)

By depicting the program as the "Infinite Chance Act," Gohmert implies that prisoners are being coddled under the Act's provisions. Representative Gohmert was not alone in opposing the legislation. Representative John Carter, like Gohmert a Republican from Texas, also spoke out against the Second Chance Act.

> I would like to ask a couple of questions. This Second Chance Act is a very new concept in criminal justice from my viewpoint. When you point out that we are actually going to create a series of benefits for people who have committed felony crimes that are not available to the average American citizen, not even available to those people who stand in harm's way and stand on the wall to protect our Nation every night from harm, and yet they are going to be available to people who commit acts, felony acts, punishable by long terms in the penitentiary. (2007, p. H5284)

In this passage, Carter sets up a pyramid of status with the military personnel at the peak, followed by the "average American citizen." At the bottom are the felons, whose needs, apparently, are to be met only after those above are satisfied. Carter continues Gohmert's attempts to frame the issue of prisoner re-entry funding as a binary between the men and women in the military and those behind bars. They are joined by Rep. Marsha Blackburn (R-TN), who made the following observation about the Second Chance Act:

> It is a matter of priorities, Mr. Speaker, and how unfortunate that the frivolous nature of some of the legislation that has come before us, that has consumed the time of this body, would be placed as a priority above the legislation to get funding to our troops in the field. And our soldiers are running out of cash. This effort is running out of cash, and we are in a global war on terror, and it is imperative that we get that money where it needs to be to those troops. (2007, H5286)

These three representatives had several commonalities beyond their opposition to the Act. One was their ideology. In addition to being Southern and from the same party, they were also members of the Republican Study Committee, an informal caucus within the party whose mission was to maintain and foster "conservative values." These values are reflected in the three member's voting records, which averaged over 90% on the pro-business U.S. Chamber of Commerce voting evaluation; and in the single digits on the pro-labor AFL-CIO analysis. Gohmert has been noted for his "fervent conservatism" while Carter and Blackburn have been called "free-market loving" and "zealous" respectively when it comes to opposing government social programs (Congressional Quarterly, 2005). What is notable about these three legislators is the remarkable similarity between their arguments against the Second Chance Act and the arguments given forth by the opponents of prisoner Pell Grants fifteen years earlier. Gohmert et al attempt to drive a rhetorical wedge between prisoners and those on the outside. As in the Pell grant debates, the Second Chance opponents attempt to portray prisoners in a state of privilege relative to other citizens. In the case of the Pell grants, prisoners go to the "head of the line" when grants are handed out. In the more recent debate, funding for prisoners, at the time estimated to average about $225 total for each one, is magnified by Gohmert, Carter, and Blackburn to suggest prisoner privilege as exemplified by the following exchange between Carter and Gohmert:

> Mr. Carter. I apologize to my colleague, Mr. Gohmert. I didn't hear all of the benefits because I came in on the tail-end, but you and I have talked about this briefly. But this training and finding jobs benefit, would that include being able to get a grant to say attend the University of Texas or your beloved Texas A&M University?

> Mr. Gohmert. It will provide training education grants. It is open-ended enough, that is a possibility, yes.

> Mr. Carter. So you could apply for a grant to attend the college or university of your choice?

> Mr. Gohmert. There are organizations that could apply for the grants to assist in that education, yes. (2007, p. H5284)

It is highly doubtful that $225 would pay for a single class at the Congressman's "beloved" university, much less a degree. Yet in the world they are constructing, the Act would provide a gateway into the highest levels of privilege to the undeserving felons. In addition to setting up a chasm between prisoners and students, Gohmert and company try to polarize the ex-prisoner unemployment and the "legitimately" unemployed as in this excerpt from Gohmert:

> Now, if you are a law-abiding citizen and you do not like your field of employment, you have to scrape together enough money to also go to school or be retrained in order to find another job. Not so under this bill if you commit a heinous crime. If you go to prison, there is grant money in this bill, not merely to train you in prison; but after you get out, there is grant money. We can retrain you every time you want to change jobs. We can pay grant money to agencies to find you new jobs. (2007, p. H5284)

The similarities between the Second Chance opponents' rhetoric and that of the Pell grant opponents' does not end with their attempts at Othering prisoners. For just as fifteen years earlier they tried to create a totalizing myth regarding the police officer who was denied financial aid due to the greed of incarcerated students, so do Gohmert and his colleagues describe a world in which military personnel are denied benefits because of funding going to prisoner re-entry. In both cases the debaters attempted to set up the most rigid binary possible by pitting the women and men in prison, often society's most vilified individuals, against the most valorized. With the Pell grant debates it was Prisoners versus Police. The police officers were sacrificing themselves on the frontlines of the War on Crime. Fifteen years later, there were additional wars going on in Afghanistan and Iraq; and police officers had been replaced with a new hero, the fighting soldier. When it came time to construct a myth of Us versus Them, the prisoners were then pitted against those who were on the front lines of the War on Terror. Gohmert opened his remarks on the Second Chance Act with the following statement:

Mr. Speaker, as always, it is such an honor to be part of this body when you know the sacrifices that have been made by so many just to allow us to be here at this time in history. There is a defense bill that we will be talking about some in the next 60 minutes.

As a former judge, I know well that we have got to do a better job of rehabilitating, of educating, with drug treatment and alcohol treatment for those that are incarcerated in our prisons. There is just no question that we should do a better job with those things. Unfortunately, this well-meaning bill, the Second Chance Act, goes so far beyond what is helpful. This bill will provide more benefits to felons than are available to those risking their lives in the service of our United States military. (2007, p. H5283)

Members of Congress were acutely aware that the nation was on wartime footing. By setting up a binary opposition between the prisoners and the military personnel, Gohmert and gang positioned prisoners as unpatriotic and themselves as being on the side of Country. Nationalism has a long history as a means of negative-other presentation and in this instance it was too much of a temptation for the rightist Republicans to pass up in their attempts at gaining hegemony. Another similarity between the debates of the two eras is the warning given regarding the threat posed by the prisoners on the moral fiber of their opposites. In the Pell grant debates the opponents warned that the police officer may turn to a life of crime in order to obtain the financial aid denied him by the incarcerated student. The Second Chance Act debate includes the following passage from Gohmert:

I was in the United States Army for 4 years, and I can tell you that unless you retire with over 20 years of active military service or you are disabled as a result of your military service, you have no medical care waiting for you at the end of your service. That means if a military member who serves less than 20 years wants a chance at free medical, he will need to commit a serious enough crime to get him locked up. (2007, p. H5283)

Just like the cop described in the Pell Grant debates who must turn to crime to obtain an education so may the serviceman have to succumb to moral temptation in order to receive medical care, all because of those prisoners who may receive some medical care as they transition back into their communities (keeping in mind this six months of medical care is being funded out of the same $225 average total per prisoner that is paying for other re-entry services).

Gohmert, Carter and Blackburn were not in office in 1993 during the Pell Grant debates, so the similarity between the rhetorical arguments may not be chalked up to recycling. This lack of personnel continuity suggests the possibility of institutional bias towards world building that constructs myths regarding Us and Them. In comparing the prisoner education opponents' tropes, it appears there's a tendency to pit the Outsiders, in this case the prisoners, against the Insiders, who are the law-abiding citizens with the stipulation that their interests are oppositional. The mythmaking involves the rhetorical positioning of a protagonist who represents society's standard-bearers of virtue as representative of all law-abiding stakeholders. Playing the role of the protagonist in the 1993 tale was the police officer. Fifteen years later it was the military serviceman. A commonality of the plot was the temptation protagonists faced when offered the choice between committing a crime and doing without education or healthcare. The instigators of this moral quandary were the prisoner and their co-conspirators in Congress.

Alas, while the attempt at constructing a myth of prisoners taking educational resources away from law abiding citizens worked in 1993, fifteen years later it ran into a much more powerful meta-narrative: the economy.

Second Chance Act Proponents

Supporters of the Second Chance Act utilized a multitude of strategies to gain votes for the bill, including economic, crime control and even compassion. There may be several reasons for this range of strategies. Proponents of the Act ranged from liberal and moderate Democrats to moderate and conservative Republicans. The diversity of the proponents played in stark contrast to the small core of hardcore conservative Republicans who opposed the legislation. Different arguments would appeal to the various representatives' ideological standpoints. Additionally, the Second Chance Act is broad-ranging legislation that included initiatives such as prisoner services facilitated through public/private partnerships with faith-based organizations.

<u>Us and Us</u>
Some of the representatives who favored prisoner re-entry programs sought to counter opponent's attempts to marginalize the women and men behind bars. One of the ways they tried to bring former prisoners back to the center was through civic education. As previously described, the majority of states place severe restrictions on prisoner voting rights. The process of re-enfranchisement tends to be very complicated in these states, often beyond the means of the average former inmate struggling to survive on the outside. Representative Gwen Moore (D-WI) calls this disenfranchisement "akin to the civic death penalty" (2007, p.H13579). One of the provisions of the Second Chance Act stipulated that upon exiting the system, prisoners must receive civics education on their basic voting rights, as described by Senator Arlen Specter (R-PA):

> The New York Times recently reported that 5 million people, or roughly 2.3 percent of the electorate, will be barred from voting in November by State laws that strip felons of voting rights. However many ex-felons are in fact eligible to vote but do not do so simply because they are not aware that they have this right. The Enhanced Second Chance Act helps remove the confusion and mandates that prison officials provide each ex-offender released from Federal prison information on how the reentering offender can restore his or her voting rights. Information must be provided to each ex-offender in writing and in a language that he or she can understand. This will allow ex-offenders to feel more connected to their communities and is another important tool in the fight to reduce recidivism. (2004, p. S10724)

Proponents of prisoner's civics education utilized the issue of disenfranchisement as a means to describe both the totality of prisoner marginalization (as shown by Moore's statement) and the ability of ex-felons to reintegrate into citizenship. Here is an example from Representative Charles Rangel (D-NY):

> The denial of black and Latino ex-felons from membership and participation in our electorate is a glaring disgrace to a country that prides itself on its equitable criminal justice system. It is said that once prisoners have ``paid their debt to society," they are free to re-enter it. But are they truly free? The answer is no if some of their fundamental rights aren't restored at the conclusion of their sentence. Not only are some ex-felons not allowed to vote, but employers hesitate to contract workers with criminal records and participation in certain housing and training programs is elusive to them as well. It is shameful and unfair to punish ex-felons even after they have served their sentence. We must avail to these citizens every opportunity to regain their dignity so they do not return to a life of crime. (2006, p. E 237)

In this passage, Rangel employs several counter-hegemonic strategies. First, he states America's dirty little secret that the vast majority of its incarcerated men and women are people of color. He further problematizes the dominant narrative by calling into question the country's claim to "equality and justice for all" within the construct of race. Rangel also unpacks what he suggests is a common misconception that prisoners face few barriers to re-engagement with non-prison life. Finally, the Congressman is one of the few, on either side of the prisoner education debate, to acknowledge ex-convicts as "citizens." Rangel was not alone in his attack on the hypocrisy of prisoner disenfranchisement. John Conyers (D-MI), a fellow member of the Congressional Black Caucus, used a similar rhetorical argument in support of voting rights:

> At a time when our Nation faces record low voter participation, this legislation represents an historic means of both expanding voting rights while helping to reintegrate former felons into our democratic society. The practice of many states denying voting rights to former felons represents a vestige from a time when suffrage was denied to whole classes

of our population based on race, gender, religion, national origin and property. Over the past two centuries, these restrictions, along with post-Civil War exclusions such as the poll tax and literacy requirements, have been eliminated. It is long past time that these restrictions be relegated to unenlightened history. Unfortunately, the United States continues to stand alone among the major industrialized nations in permitting an entire category of citizens, former felons, to be cut off from the democratic process. It is time that the United States restored these fundamental rights and join the community of nations in this regard…one in four black men are permanently disenfranchised. Hispanic citizens are also disproportionately disenfranchised. In addition to diminishing the legitimacy of our democratic process, denying voting rights to ex-offenders is inconsistent with the goal of rehabilitation. Instead of reintegrating such individuals into society, felony voting restrictions only serve to reaffirm their feelings of alienation and isolation. (2003, p. E40)

Representative Conyers traces prisoner alienation to its roots in the "unenlightened" past of the previous two hundred years. The disenfranchisement of inmates is placed within the context of a long history of marginalization of people of color, women, various religions, immigrants, and the poor. Thus, he establishes an important link temporally *and* spatially, between prisoner rights and past injustices and current struggles of the subaltern. Like Rangel, he exposes the disproportional impact on Blacks and Hispanics. In addition Conyers follows his New York colleague's line of dissent by calling into question American's authority as a bastion of global democracy. Conyers suggests that the way for the U.S. to reverse its "diminishing of legitimacy" would be to restore voting rights and "join the community of nations." These are important counter-hegemonic statements for they position the incarceration issue as not merely an anomaly in the criminal justice apparatus, but as a symptom of systemic problems.

Moore, Conyers, and Rangel manage to invert the paradigm of prisoners as perpetrator and society as victim by deftly pointing out the hypocrisy in denying these citizens their rights to civic engagement.

However, there was not complete support for their position among the backers of the Second Chance Act. With such an ideologically diverse group there were bound to be some cracks. Robert Erlrich, the Republican Governor of Maryland, testified at the Congressional Hearing in favor of the Second Chance Act. However, he remained a strong opponent of restoring voting rights to prisoners, a fact pointed out by Rangel during the debate:

> Mr. Speaker, it is my hope that Gov. Ehrlich comes to realize the type of damage his vow to forbid restoration of voting rights to ex-prisoners has done to disadvantaged communities in his state. It is his vow that I find inappropriate. (2006, p. E237)

Ultimately, Rangel and company failed to convince their fellow legislators to support re-enfranchisement for the women and men convicted of crimes. The most they were able to get was a weak provision to the Second Chance Act requiring "civic education" where upon the inmate's release, the prison officials would be required to provide written information on the process involved in regaining voting rights (if re-enfranchising is allowed in the state).

The civics education mandated by the Second Chance Act appears to be narrowly focused on obtaining ballot access. There is little mention of other rights that are just as important to becoming a fully engaged citizen, including the right to advocacy and the right to organize. In addition, most jurisdictions bar convicted felons from holding elected office. The civics education contained within the Second Chance Act is indeed a modest step toward restoring the full citizenship to the two million men and women in prison and the five million ex-felons. However, given the ideological diversity of the coalition supporting the Act, narrowly defined civics education may have been the only palatable provision on this politically charged issue. That did not stop members of the Congressional Black Caucus from using the debates as a forum to problematize the marginalization of prisoners within the framework of civil rights.

<u>Family Values</u>
One of the primary differences between the rhetorical strategies of the proponents of Pell grants for prisoners and that of many Second Chance

Act proponents was the effort to frame the debate within the context of not only the women and men in prison; but their wider social lives, particularly their families. One of the leading adherents to this strategy was Representative Danny Davis (D-IL). As mentioned earlier, Davis was in the House chamber when President Bush first stated his support for the prisoner education and re-entry initiative. The Congressman recalls that he was:

> Equally elated when I received a call from then Representative Rob Portman's office inviting me to work with him to try and move toward implementation of the goal toward re-entry. (Second Chance Hearing, p. 2005, p. 12)

Davis' enthusiastic backing of the legislation as well as his ability to work with members of the opposition party such as Portman, was crucial in guiding the bill through the House Chamber. Upon the signing of the legislation he was widely recognized as a key player in its passage. Praising him were President Bush, who singled him out for recognition, and Rep. Carolyn Kilpatrick (D-MI), chairperson of the Congressional Black Caucus. Kilpatrick referred to Davis as "chief sponsor of the Second Chance Act [who] exhibited supreme social and moral consciousness in drafting this bill and the steadfastness to fight for five years to ensure passage" (Barrett, 2008, p.1).

The Second Chance Act is an effort apparently focused on the most marginalized in society. It should not come as a surprise that Davis would come down on their side given his background. Davis was born in a very poor section of segregated Arkansas in 1941. His parents were Black sharecroppers and, as a child he often had to help out in the fields picking cotton along with his eleven sisters and brothers. Consequently, Davis went to school only about four months out of the year. The Congressman appears to have kept in touch with his working class roots, being one of the few representatives in 2002 to gain a perfect, 100% positive score on the pro-union AFL-CIO voting score card and 0% on the pro-big business American Conservative Union evaluation. Although Davis' congressional district in Chicago is a mixture of high-income suburbs and low income projects, he seems to have made a commitment to keep his priorities straight. Davis chose to focus on prisoner education "rather than run from it, or hope someone else will do it" (Congressional Quarterly, 2005, p. 342).

In his defense of the Second Chance Act, Davis gave the following statement on the House floor on May 23rd of 2007:

> Mr. Speaker, I am convinced that any serious effort to facilitate the reentry of men and women with criminal records to civil society must be prepared to do two things. First, we must be prepared to help with drug treatment on demand for everyone who requests it. (2007, p. H5691)

In this passage, the Congressman appears to unpack some of the institutional mores that bind prisoners to the margins. He describes drug treatment as a right, not a privilege by suggesting that a "serious" effort to help recently released prisoners must include treatment "on demand for everyone who requests it." Inherent in this proposition, is a recognition of agency in the women and men. Unlike some legislators, who have suggested that former drug offenders be required to seek treatment as a condition of release, Davis appears to weaken the barriers that arise in "totalizing" institutions. Barriers that achieve a subjection of the participants even as they are "released" from control. These include conditions of parole or probation that exist and are perceived by the "subjects" as impediments to their ability to act as free agents in their own construction of identity. Having been classified as drug addicts and required to seek treatment, the former prisoner is still perceived as the perpetual Other – released from prison, but not part of free society.

In another excerpt, Davis seeks to unpack one of the foundational "truths" of society's views of criminals: That of the sociopath, incapable of existing within relationships beyond those of perpetrator and victim:

> The vast majority, 95 percent, of the men and women in our prisons will eventually return to the community. This means that every year more than 650,000 offenders are released from State and Federal prisons and return back to civilian life. These men and women deserve a second chance. Their

families, spouses, and children deserve a second chance. And their communities deserve a second chance. (2007, p. H5691)

Like a pebble dropped in a pond, the Congressman's words evoke a prisoner's world as ever-widening concentric circles. The convict is a woman or a man, who may have families, such as a father or mother and a spouse and/or son or daughter. As the circles widen, they include their communities and friends throughout their neighborhoods. In Davis' world, the women and men in prison are not just criminals. That designation does not represent their totality. They exist in a multifaceted plane that relates to their status as human beings, capable of forming complex relationships, of loving and being loved.

The placement of prisoners within the context of family and community was an oft-used theme during Second Chance Act debates. Here is an example from then-Senator Barack Obama (D-IL):

This year, approximately 650,000 prisoners will be released into communities across America communities in which all of us live. They will have paid their debt to society and will now return to their homes and neighborhoods, to their families, and back to their lives. Their communities are our communities; their success is an important part of our success as a larger community and a nation. The problem is that for most of these men--and more than 9 out of 10 of them are men--their families, neighborhoods, and prior lives often lack what it takes to ensure successful reintegration. If we punish crime, as we should, then we must also recognize that when punishment is concluded, there are lives that must be resumed constructively. We only hurt ourselves and our own communities if we fail. That is why the Second Chance Act is so important. It is the leading edge of a smart community response to the challenges we all face from this inevitable feature of our justice system. In the best of cases, incarcerated individuals maintain contact with their families and receive rehabilitation services while in prison; they are released to a network of law-abiding peers and quickly find a rewarding job that provides the skills and career development for long-term opportunity. Released prisoners can help support their families, become active in their churches and other community organizations, stay off drugs, away from trouble, on track, and out of jail. Unfortunately, that rarely happens. Up to two-thirds of all released prisoners nationwide end up back in prison within just 3 years. That means that of the 1,800 people released from prisons every single day in this country, almost 1,200 fail to make a successful transition into the world of work and responsibility. They do not manage to find and keep effective jobs and to care for themselves and their families. Many become a drain on their families and a drain on the system. They are more likely to resort to criminal activity and to perpetuate poverty and family dysfunction. And their failure is our failure since we all share the high cost and other burdens of unemployment, crime, community failure, and cycles of recidivism. (2005, p. S12521)

Whereas the opponents of prisoner education established an essentializing narrative of prisoners solely defined within the construct of their criminal activities, Obama, like Davis in the previous passage, attempts to widen the lens in which men and women behind bars are viewed. The circles ripple out to include family, neighbor and community. In order to emphasize his point, the Senator riffs on the term "family" seven times. The idea of community is repeated nine times in this passage. In the hands of a skillful orator such as Obama, the sound of repetitive phrases can carry a phonological force that extends beyond the elocutionary effect of the actual words. This was a speech that was meant to be heard.

Why the emphasis on family and community? Obama appears to be utilizing a strategy similar to Representative Davis by endeavoring to problematize the marginalization of prisoners. Family and community are commonalities that exist across cultures and subcultures. By placing the women and men in prison within that shared experience of familial relations, the Senator weaves a connection that potentially can be understood by all within the audience. To emphasize this point, Obama includes the phrase "Their communities are our communities; their success is an important part of our success" and "their failure is our failure." Obama built a career that eventually led to the White House in part on the rhetoric (and often the reality) of inclusivity. He brought his considerable speaking skills to bear in his effort to deconstruct the notion of criminals as Other.

Charles Rangel (D-NY) emphasized the obstacles faced by former prisoners as they seek to re-enter their communities:

> One-third of all correction departments provide no services to released offenders, and most departments do not offer a transitional program, placing a heavy burden on families and communities. Most men and women released face tremendous obstacles as they try to reenter society successfully, encountering imposing impediments to attaining gainful employment, overcoming drug addictions, gaining custody of their children, or finding affordable housing. In fact, two-thirds of those released will be arrested within three years of leaving prison (2007, p. E1506).

Rangel recognizes there is substantial societal resistance to integration of these men and women back into their communities. Finding a job or a domicile can be problematic even for someone without a criminal record, but with background checks and regulatory prohibitions against living in public housing, those who have committed crimes are virtually locked out of support systems. These support systems, which may be family-based or community-based are often inaccessible if that family lives in public housing or the former inmate's community has a high unemployment rate. The problem becomes even more acute if the parent has to fight to regain custody of a child lost due to imprisonment. As Rangel points out, the returnee then becomes a "burden" on the family and community, a status that raises the risk of alienation in a time of need.

In this passage, Rangel flips the paradigm established by Davis and Obama. Whereas the latter two emphasize the status of the prisoners and former prisoners as part of a broader society embedded in family, neighborhoods and community, Rangel describes the feedback mechanism whereby the impediments to access to the very societal structures to which they are a part accentuates the risk of marginalization. Rather than problematizing Davis and Obama's valuations, Rangel complements them.

<u>Faith-based Arguments</u>
In the same State of the Union address in which President Bush expressed his support for a Second Chance Act, he laid out his vision for a heightened role for religious institutions in helping to facilitate government social services:

> It's also important to strengthen our communities by unleashing the compassion of America's religious institutions. Religious charities of every creed are doing some of the most vital work in our country: mentoring children, feeding the hungry, taking the hand of the lonely. Yet government has often denied social-service grants and contracts to these groups just because they have a cross or a Star of David or a crescent on the wall. By executive order, I have opened billions of dollars in grant money to competition that includes faith-based charities. Tonight I ask you to codify this into law so people of faith can know that the law will never discriminate against them again. (State of the Union Address, 2004, p.2)

Bush's call for faith-based initiatives within the construct of the state was not new. His opponent in the 2000 presidential race, Al Gore, also pledged that "if you elect me President, the voices of faith-based organizations will be integral to the policies set forth in my administration" (Black, Koopman & Ryden, 2004 p. 76). It was Bush who sought a "fundamental" change in the role religious institutions have in the workings of the government. This paradigmatic change would include the establishment of an office of faith-based initiatives which would facilitate church/state relationships as well as massive re-channeling of funding away from government social programs toward faith-based social service organizations.

Advocates of faith-based initiatives point out that the initiatives facilitate the welding of private and government activities that are of the same goal, thus reducing redundancy and bureaucratic overhead. Religious organizations have been viewed as the conscience of a nation. Faith-based initiatives are touted as a means to give these groups a greater voice both in policy decisions as well as a role in the enactment of the policies. In addition, the initiatives have been viewed as a conduit for the marginalized, such as the poor, to influence policy since their participation in religious institutions is often greater than other societal bodies, thus providing a forum for them to advocate their agendas (Formicola, Segers & Weber, 2003).

Critics of faith-based public/private partnerships, such as Robert Wineburg (2007) suggest several aspects of the policy are problematic. A fundamental drawback is the apparent compromise of the separation of church and state provisions in the U.S. Constitution, where it is specifically forbidden for government to establish and promote a religious viewpoint. He also points out that the temptation would exist for the political establishment to privilege the dominant religious ideology in order to further its electoral and/or spiritual agenda. The Bush Administration has been accused of providing greater access and funding to Christian organizations, particularly those associated with fundamentalism. A litmus test of what is deemed acceptable spiritual social services is often applied. He also suggests that Bush's faith-based initiative correlates with the Administration's broader political ideology by serving as a means to reduce the role of the State. This is accomplished by downsizing government agencies and shifting welfare services to the Church as part of an "individualistic message" of what constitutes charity (Wineburg, 2007 p. 118). Sharp (2010) has suggested a link between Bush's establishment of the Office of Faith-based and Community Initiatives (OFBCI) and neoliberal economic policy, "it must be noted that the OFBCI emerged amid diminishing of opportunity for the federal government to reinforce and to expand social programs because of the ascendancy of neoliberalism" (P. 55).

When President Bush first outlined his plan for the Second Chance Act he called for a "four-year, $300 million Prison Re-entry Initiative to expand job training and placement services, to provide transitional housing and to help newly released prisoners get mentoring, *including from faith-based groups*" (emphasis added) (State of the Union Address, 2004, p.2).

The Second Chance Act legislation included key faith-based elements. Among these were provisions setting up public/private partnerships between the State and religious organizations to help with prisoner re-integration. The legislation's text called upon the Department of Corrections to:

> Coordinate and collaborate with other Federal agencies and with State, Tribal, and local criminal justice agencies, community-based organizations, and faith-based organizations to help effectuate a seamless reintegration of prisoners into communities. (Second Chance Act, 2007, p. H13572)

The bill also authorizes funding to faith-based and community non-profit groups to provide services to prisoners including, "prison mentoring programs through which church members and community members provide individualized mentoring to prisoners who want to turn their lives around" (Specter, 2008, p. S1993).

Not surprisingly, religious organizations lined up in support of the Second Chance Act. They included the American Catholic Correctional Chaplains Association; Correctional Chaplains Association; Catholic Charities USA; Christian Coalition; Church Women United; Covenant House; Evangelical Lutheran Church in America; Family Research Council; Horizon Faith-based Communities in Prisons, Jewish Prisoner Services International; Prisoner Fellowship; Lutheran Services of America; Mennonite Central Committee; National Alliance of Faith and Justice; National Black Church Taskforce Initiative on Crime and Criminal Justice; National Religious Affairs Association; Presbyterian Church (USA); National Baptist Convention, USA; Salvation Army; Samaritan Village; United Church of Christ/Justice and Witness Ministries; United Methodist General Board of Church and Society; United States Conference of Catholic Bishops; Women of Reform Judaism and the World of Hope Ministries (Brownback, 2008, S2938).

The list includes a fairly wide spectrum of Christian organizations ranging from the far right Christian Coalition and Family Research Council to the more moderate/ progressive United Church of Christ and the Mennonite Central Committee. The legistation's endorsers, although overwhelmingly Christian, include two Jewish organizations. Notably absent were any organizations that were Muslim centered or from the Religious Society of Friends (Quakers). These absences are conspicuous because Muslims have had a presence in prisons since the 1960s (Conley & Debro, 2002). Quakers have an even longer history of prison ministry and reform, dating back to some of the early

American prisons and jails (Welch, 1996; Bosworth, 2010). They continue to this day to be active in prison reform.

Chief congressional sponsors of the Second Chance Act included the Democrats, Danny Davis and Joe Biden, as well as the Republicans, Chris Cannon and Sam Brownback. The latter two tend to be reliably conservative in opposing government-run social programs, yet they are strong supporters of the President's faith-based initiative.

During the course of the legislative debate, supporters of the Second Chance Act utilized religious references in a manner unseen in the Pell grant debates. Some of the rhetoric included relatively subtle uses of religion-associated terminology as in the excerpt below from remarks given by Representative Sheila Jackson-Lee (D-TX).

> Releasing rehabilitated, middle-aged, nonviolent offenders from an already overcrowded prison population can be a win-win situation for society and the individual who, like the Jean Valjean made famous in Victor Hugo's Les Miserables, is redeemed by the grace of a second chance. The reentry of such individuals into the society will enable them to repay the community through community service and obtain or regain a sense of self-worth and accomplishment. It promises a reduction in burdens to the taxpayer, and an affirmation of the American value that no nonviolent offender is beyond redemption. (2007, p. E2597)

In her description of the prisoner, typified by Jean Valjean, the person is 'redeemed" and is not "beyond redemption." These are terms that are often applied to the Christian vision of the sinner who has found his way back to the path of righteousness and is redeemed through faith. Jackson-Lee fortifies this association by bringing in the word "grace," which is usually associated with the granting of a state of Salvation. The believer is "saved" by the grace of the Supreme Being. Adding to the association is the term "affirmation," a term typically utilized in the Church as descriptor of the public display of belief. From a pragmatic's perspective, given the faith-based content of the legislation, the terms' association with religion is likely the intention of the speech.

Much of the debate included overt invocation of Christian scripture as in the following excerpt from Representative Stephanie Tubbs-Jones (D- OH), a member of the Congressional Black Caucus:

> Last week we were talking about reading the Bible, the week of the Bible and how important it was to follow God's word. What more important? [sic] God said you visited me when I was sick, when I was in jail. Second Chance can do that. (2007, H13579)

Tubbs-Jones makes a reference to National Bible Week and pulls it into context of the legislation by pointing out a specific passage from the book of Matthew, chapter 25, verse 36 which reads: "Naked and ye clothed me; I was sick and ye visited me; I was in prison and ye came unto me" (King James version, n.d.). The Representative does not need to specify that she is taking her excerpt from the Christian bible, nor does she feel the need to provide the verse from which it is taken, for these details already exist within the lived culture of many members of Congress (and a good portion of America for that matter). The assumptions are part of the collocational relationships that provide force to her speech. In other words, the fact that there exists implied understanding that the listener knows (or should know) the full context of the biblical reference provides added currency to its use. Tubbs-Jones was not alone in the use of scripture. Representatives Davis and Jackson-Lee made frequent references to verses and parables from the Christian bible in their support of the Act. Nor was the tactic limited to the proponents as evidenced by the following statement from Louie Gohmert (R-TX):

> And when we talk about Scripture, absolutely, there are all kinds of verses that apply to us for those that believe the teachings of Jesus as I do. They are entirely appropriate. Those are directed to individuals. If you get over to Romans 13, that is directed to the government. And where it says if you do evil, you need to be afraid, because God does not give the government the sword in vain, that is part of the role of government; if you do evil, then there are consequences. (2007, p. H13580)

This passage was apparently in direct response to Tubbs-Jones' biblical reference, for Gohmert earlier prefaced it by stating "I do appreciate Mrs. Tubbs-Jones' comments." In Gohmert's response, he seems to narrow the scope of believers by saying "there are all kinds of verses that apply to *us* for those that believe the teachings of Jesus as I do" [emphasis added]. The implication is that the scripture applies to "us," but believer is "I," thus singling himself out as the true believer, even though the dogma also applies to others. As he is *the* believer, he seems to imply his interpretation of the scripture's true meaning is foundational and universally applicable.

The biblical passage to comfort the prisoner, in Gohmert's world is "directed to individuals" whereas when it comes to the state, Gohmert asserts that "God does not give the government the sword in vain, that is part of the role of government; if you do evil, then there are consequences." Gohmert's scriptural interpretation appears to provide a perfect biblical justification for his political standpoint: Helping the poor, the sick and the imprisoned are within the domain of the *individual's* religious responsibilities, while the role of the State, whom God has given the sword, is to punish lawbreakers.

While a true believer such as Louie Gohmert, apparently has no difficulty reconciling the political and religious belief systems with opposition to prisoner education, what about the conservatives who supported the Second Chance Act? President Bush, in his State of the Union address, seemed to weave a neat justification for the massive federal program by touting its faith base. Conservative Republicans in the Senate, such as Sam Brownback (R- KS) and Rick Santorum (R-PA) had a long history of opposing public expenditures for social programs, yet they were ardent proponents of the Second Chance Act. So was Representative Chris Cannon (R-UT).

Chris Cannon, in many ways is a consummate House Republican having ridden in on the conservative wave that brought Newt Gingrich to power in the mid-1990s. Cannon's early claim to fame was his dogged efforts to have then-President Bill Clinton impeached. His voting record scorecards have been reliably conservative according to the AFL-CIO and American Conservative Union. The one area where he has strayed from the right has been in his support for liberalizing immigration policy. Cannon justifies this stand by citing his experiences as a young Mormon missionary in Central America. This excuse may serve him well in his home district which is conservative and has a large population of Mormons (Congressional Quarterly, 2005).

Cannon is not shy about laying his religious beliefs on the table as indicated from the following section of a statement given at a House hearing on the Second Chance Act.

> I think this is a fundamentally moral issue, and in America, we have a religion. Much has been written about that. It is not one sect or another, but there are some fundamental ideas that we hold as Americans, fundamental religious ideas, and at the base of that is the belief that there is a god" (Second Chance Hearing, 2005, p. 9).

Here he expresses a philosophy that is based in Christian fundamentalism (he even uses the latter word several times), that there exists a common belief system a religion, that, in his view defines one's position as an American. He then describes the imperative dictated by this value system to help those who are incarcerated. "You don't find a statement where we are mandated to take care of those less fortunate without including the concept of prisoners. And that's because prisoners are human beings that God cares about and that we are going to be judged as to how we deal with them" (Second Chance Hearing, 2005, p. 9).

Cannon continues in the fundamentalist Christian vein with the pronouncement that those who deny support to prisoners risk a negative outcome on Judgment Day. In a separate speech given on the House floor, the Representative repeats much of his fundamentalist rhetoric:

> After Mr. Portman left Congress, I took over as the primary sponsor and this Congress I cosponsored this legislation for the reasons I have stated. I believe there are some fundamental ideas that we hold as Americans. The first is that there is a God and that we will all at some point face divine judgment. You don't have to believe in God to be an American, but most Americans, believers or not, when given a choice will support limiting government to promote the

welfare of their fellow man. For believers like me, this legislation does that. (2007, H13582)

Cannon begins by laying claim to the position as the legislation's chief sponsor, a claim roundly disputed by Danny Davis' cohorts. Secondly, he like Gohmert, provides a narrative that ties his religious values to his policy stands. Like his fellow Republican, Cannon states his support for a diminished role for government in providing "welfare." However, unlike his colleague, he states that the Second Chance Act serves as a vehicle to accomplish that aim. This excerpt appears to reconcile the seeming contradiction between an anti-big-government philosophy and supporting a new, 300 million dollar federal program. It appears that the Representative agrees with the assertion (previously described by Wineburg) that faith-based programs can serve as a means to downsize government's social service responsibilities by "limiting government."

<u>Economic Policy</u>
 Much of the debate over the Second Chance Act centered upon the economic savings the government would realize as a result of releasing inmates. Congress by constitutional authority is the steward of the federal budget. Providing funding for a specific federal mandate is a lengthy process involving budget and appropriations committees as well as conference committees that serve to reconcile differences between House and Senate appropriations (Congressional Quarterly, 2008). Authorizing and appropriating spending are separate processes and many pieces of legislation that have contained specific targets for funds for a federal service, have ended up as ineffectual because the money was never actually provided. Hence, this explains the frequency of "unfunded mandates." The control over the purse strings provides Congress a great deal of power. According to Vile (2007): "Laws must be enforced, policies must be implemented, and they always cost money. The raising and spending of money provides the ultimate control by Congress over the administration" (p. 141). This is a privilege that members of Congress cherish and one that is often used to their own advantage by providing a means to funnel tax dollars to their own districts. Consequently, attempts to reduce their authority over budgeting have met with strong resistance: "Congress has been

tenacious in its bid to retain the ultimate control, rejecting all proposals that would loosen its hold on the purse strings" (p. 141).

As a result of its budgetary responsibilities, debate over legislation that requires expenditures often contains discourse centered on discussion of the cost effectiveness of the law. In the debate over denial of Pell Grants for prisoners, several opponents attempted to shape the issue in context of overall budgetary constraints. A similar tactic was utilized by some in opposition to the Second Chance Act as previously described. With the costs of massive incarceration escalating, those who advocated prisoner education and re-entry saw an opportunity to frame the issue as a "common sense" tradeoff between spending on the prisoner's room, board and oversight or on the relatively modest costs of the Second Chance Act education and other re-entry services. As stated earlier, the Act budgeted about $225 average a year for each man and woman estimated to be released over the two years following passage. In the following, Representative Bill Delahunt (D-MA) points out the budgetary advantages of the legislation:

> Common sense dictates that here is part of an answer, part of an answer to increase safety within our communities. So it should not be unanticipated or unexpected that two former prosecutors like Stephanie and myself should be ardent advocates for this approach, because it does make sense, and it enhances public safety. And again, it relieves the burden, if you will, on a criminal justice system that has difficulty finding resources to simply process people through. And that's not healthy for the criminal justice system. (Second Chance Hearing, 2005, p. 53)

Delahunt portrays his viewpoint as a "common sense" choice between crime and safety and as a matter of being wise stewards of the taxpayer's dollars. By freeing up funding from incarceration costs, the communities will then have "healthy" criminal justice systems. Delahunt was not alone in pointing out the Second Chance Act as a rational choice. Representative Barbara Lee (D-CA) utilized a very similar line of thought in her speech:

> Prisoner reentry is not a Democratic issue. It is not a
> Republican issue. It is a common sense issue. The facts are
> clear--meaningful reentry programs significantly diminish the
> chances that ex-offenders will return to prison. That saves
> taxpayer dollars and increases public safety. So why not invest
> in enhancing reentry programs in order to end the cycle of
> recidivism? That is exactly what the Second Chance Act does.
> (2007, p. H8283)

The Representative expands on Delahunt's argument by describing the commonality by naming both the Republican and Democratic parties within the framework of the two Democrats' thesis. The legislation contains elements that appeal to all concerned as a "win-win" situation. Elements that appeal to the Democrats on the Left include the establishment of a social program to help manage those problems of society's most marginalized groups while Republicans and centrist Democrats see an opportunity to cut the budget without compromising public safety. Of course these problems overlap in that those on the Left also may have concerns over crime and fiscal responsibility, but not usually within a formula for addressing the issues that would please the Republicans. By creating legislation that brings together multifaceted standpoints within a "common sense" framework and creating a world in which these commonalities are privileged over other concerns, each stakeholder also "wins." The space of common concern arises by each participant making the rational choice to set aside partisanship. Representative Howard Coble (R-NC) put the issue succinctly when he said:

> At the heart of this matter is a simple calculation: will the
> economic and societal savings of reduced recidivism be
> greater than the cost of the resources needed to allow
> individuals returning to society to make this transition
> successfully? Research has shown that the answer to this
> simple calculation is yes. (Second Chance Hearing, 2005, p. 1)

In his world, the issue of prisoner re-entry comes down to a simple question of cost/benefits. This is the "heart of the matter" and the heart supplies all parts of the body politic. Without it, other concerns are superfluous. Questions of compassion and altruism are secondary and not a function in the calculation as the representative perceives the problems as a "simple" matter of social and economic exchange.

Given their focus on the bottom line, it should not come as a surprise that many of the members of Congress view prisoners within the same narrow lens. An indicator of this view is found within the wording of the Second Chance Act:

> (2) Measuring The Removal Of Obstacles To Reentry.--
> (A) Coding Required.--The Director shall ensure that each institution within the Bureau of Prisons codes the reentry needs and deficits of prisoners, as identified by an assessment tool that is used to produce an individualized skills development plan for each inmate.
> (B) Tracking.--In carrying out this paragraph, the Director shall quantitatively track the progress in responding to the reentry needs and deficits of individual inmates.
> (C) Annual Report.--On an annual basis, the Director shall prepare and submit to the Committee on the Judiciary of the Senate and the Committee on the Judiciary of the House of Representatives a report that documents the progress of the Bureau of Prisons in responding to the reentry needs and deficits of inmates. (2007, p. H13572)

This section of the Act pertains to the Federal Bureau of Prisons and calls upon it to classify the prisoners and then track their trajectory using quantitative data. A key aspect of the passage is the description of the prisoners. They are described as having "needs," which implied a lack of both strengths and agency. Needs are analogous to a negative pressure that is directed inward. The women and men are perceived as only capable of receiving, not giving, which requires agency. Whatever skills, abilities, intelligences, acumen, and/or talents they may have are not seen as strengths that can radiate outward in a positive direction. Instead, they are either discounted in the equation or characterized as "deficits" which need to be eliminated and replaced. Additionally, because they have "needs" but not wants, the wants of the men and women are discounted in the data. What do the re-entering prisoners desire? What would they like to study? What occupation do they want? How do they see their community and their place in its future? These are important questions that may not be addressed within an institutional formula that narrowly focuses upon deficit.

Despite the legislation's narrow view of prisoners, in the debates, many of the Representatives' speeches focused on their potential to become "productive" and "contributing" members of society, as in this excerpt from Senator Biden:

> We also need to examine existing Federal and state reentry barriers--laws, regulations, rules, and practices that make it more difficult for former inmates to successfully reintegrate back into their communities; laws that confine ex-offenders to society's margins, making it even more likely that they will recommit serious crimes and return to prison. Turning over a new leaf and going from a life of crime to becoming a productive member of society is tough enough. We shouldn't have Federal and State laws on the books that make this even more challenging. (2004, p. S10718)

The Senator never really defines what is meant by productive. Is it being economically productive, as in being part of the labor force as a worker or artisan and providing a product for consumers? Or is it by becoming an entrepreneur or manager who has others do the building for their creations? Perhaps productivity can include those in the retail sector who sell the product or even the service sector which provides for the wants and needs of all of the above groups. Are there other ways of being productive that do not fit within the framework of the market? Within the lived culture of Congress, there appears to be little need to clarify what is meant by productive; and the instances of members using the term "productive members of society" without explanation abound both within the Pell Grant debates as well as those over the Second Chance Act. However, the term productive is almost always given within the context of economics as in the following passage from a speech by Representative Elijah Cummings (D-MD):

> We stand to save billions of taxpayer dollars by reducing recidivism rates by steering our ex-offenders away from a life of crime and into a productive society. (2007, p. H13829)

Productive former inmates are often seen as the end result of an "investment" by society as illustrated by Representative Bobby Scott of Virginia's excerpt:

> This saves money and reduces crime so that the law-abiding citizen doesn't have to worry as much about being a victim of crime. You do that by helping the prisoner lead a productive life. That is what your bill does. It is cost effective and reduces crime. (2005, p. H11095)

In keeping with his persuasive argument, he acknowledges the benefits of the bill in saving money and this is the context in which he places the "productive" former prisoner.

In a statement given at the Congressional Hearing on the Second Chance Act, Representative Tubbs-Jones describes the story of Derrick, a young man who went through a state-run re-entry program in the Congressperson's home district. Derrick was a multiple offender on charges ranging from drugs to burglary before becoming involved with the Community-oriented Re-entry Program (CORE). In the following passage, Tubbs-Jones describes the impact of the program on the young man.

> Between the ages of 16 and 24, Derrick was incarcerated six times for a variety of offenses (drugs, theft, burglary, etc). During his sixth incarceration he was introduced to the CORE program and the Reentry Management Team. At first, his level of maturity did not seem to extend beyond that of a teenager. His body language and demeanor still reflected a street mentality and the "law of survival." However, to the surprise of the team, Derrick not only successfully completed the CORE program and his incarceration, but upon his release to the community and completion of his correctional supervision, he became a model client. After several weeks, he began to open up with the help of his case manager. He started to become excited about life and the opportunities ahead. Derrick was never late for any of his appointments, never tested positive for drugs, nor was he sanctioned during his supervision. He truly became a role model for his peers in

the reentry program. In May of 2004, Derrick obtained his first employment ever at Wendy's Restaurant. He took great pride in working and earning his own money. Today, he has moved on from Wendy's and is now working in construction. The pay is better, and he is excited about the opportunity to learn about the construction business. In a nutshell, Derrick's story encompasses the need to expand the support for reentry services. Without CORE, he would probably not have been able to turn his life around. He is now a productive, tax-paying citizen. (Second Chance Act, 2005, p. 16)

Within the context of the narrative of Derrick's experience with CORE, the Representative provides a glimpse into her view of what it means to be productive. In the tale, the young man redeems himself through his punctuality, ability to stay off drugs and avoidance of conflict resulting in sanctions. While these accomplishments do not fall under the category of external production, they do represent Derrick's remaking of himself. He has succeeded in re-modeling himself into an employable being that has the capability of being productive within the framework of the job market, so much so that he serves as a model for his cohorts. Derrick has succeeded in reconfiguring his identity from that of a "street mentality" to a "model client" (at least in the eyes of others). The young man began to envision the "opportunities" that his new identity offered which manifested in a restaurant job and the opportunity to learn a trade in construction. The young man had evolved from an ex-offender to a "productive, tax-paying citizen." In the narrative above, the construction of the ideal citizen has, at its end result the ability to contribute labor and a portion of its rewards to the state (to help finance the reconstruction of others). President Bush, when he signed the Second Chance Act into law, reiterated this meta-narrative by stating that:

The country was built on the belief that each human being has limitless potential and worth. Everybody matters. We believe that even those who have struggled with a dark past can find brighter days ahead. One way we act on that belief is by helping former prisoners who've paid for their crimes. We help them build new lives as productive members of our society. (Bush, 2008, p. 2)

Further in his speech, Bush provides clarity to his phrase "productive members" by stating: "The high recidivism rate places a huge financial burden on taxpayers; it deprives our labor force of *productive workers* [emphasis added]." It appears the focus of the Second Chance Act debate is on prisoners as commodities in a very narrow sense of their relationship to the labor market. The creation of this human capital requires investment in the subject. This investment comes in the form of legislation that provides funding for faith-based mentoring, transitional housing and healthcare as well as education. Education can take many forms, ranging from basic adult education and literacy to vocational training to higher education such as liberal arts. Where do the framers of the Second Chance Act place prisoner education within this spectrum?

<u>Education as Job Training</u>
The supporters of the Second Chance Act apparently had a vision of the kind of education men and women behind bars needed as indicated by this statement from Senator Specter:

> There are two categories of individuals that we must focus our concern on in our fight to reduce recidivism--the career criminal and the person who will one day return back to his or her community. As for the career criminal, I wrote the Armed Career Criminal Bill that was adopted in 1984, which provides for life sentences for career criminals. These individuals, who have committed three or more major offenses and caught in possession of a firearm, receive mandatory sentences up to life. The second category of individuals--individuals who will one day be released--are a special circumstance because this is not about locking them up forever but about making sure they have an opportunity to turn their life around. It is about focusing on literacy and job training in order to reduce recidivism and prevent those individuals from becoming career criminals. (2004, p. S10724)

In this passage the Senator attempts several goals. One is to distinguish between the incorrigible criminals and those who can be redeemed. The "career criminals" have been designated beyond redemption due to their committing at least three "major" crimes (see earlier discussion of the "three strikes you're out" trend). Thus they are situated outside of acceptable society permanently. With this passage, Specter builds at least two foundations of understanding: Firstly, that he is a tough, but fair legislator by ingraining the idea that his support of harsh laws indicates his advocacy of prisoner re-entry does not make him "soft on crime." Secondly, by creating a binary between the two classes of prisoners, Specter attempts to construct a view that not all inmates are the same. The second group is typified as "the person who will one day return back to his or her community" and has the potential to avoid crossing the boundary to the first group through education. However, it is a very specific kind of education that will "turn their life around" and that is "literacy and job training."

The ability of basic education to be transformative is a recurring theme in the Second Chance Act debates. Here is another example, this time from Senator Ted Kennedy (D-MA):

> We also cannot expect ex-offenders to become productive members of the community if they don't have the education and vocational training they need to find jobs. The Bureau of Justice Statistics reports that only 46 percent of incarcerated individuals have a high school diploma or its equivalent. The limited availability of education and vocational training programs exacerbates the problem. Only 5 percent of jail jurisdictions offer vocational training, and 33 percent of jurisdictions offer no educational or vocational training at all. (2007, p. S4431)

The Senator offers a direct link between transforming prisoners into productive members of society and their educational attainment, as well as the long term goal of finding jobs. In a further excerpt, Kennedy elaborates on the kinds of education required to achieve transformation:

The Second Chance Act supports community education and vocational training programs that have proven their effectiveness, and offers the tools and resources to study best practices on job training and placement. It also supports collaboration among community corrections, technical schools, community colleges, and the workforce development and employment service sectors to help ex-offenders overcome the many barriers they face in finding employment. (2007, S4431)

Within the learning sphere of prisoners and former prisoners, there only exists community colleges and technical schools with no mention of university-level schools. Unlike Second Chance Act opponent Gohmert, Kennedy sees value in former inmates attending school, albeit lower echelon programs that are community-based. But similar to Gohmert, who was aghast at the thought of former prisoners attending his alma mater, Texas A&M University, Kennedy also seems to see little value in prisoners obtaining an education at the university level.

Tellingly, the Second Chance Act does not lessen the restrictions on financial aid to prisoners that were codified in the 1994 Omnibus Crime Bill. They were still denied access to Pell grants. Proponents of the Act could have inserted language vacating these prohibitions, but they did not. However, the legislation does make specific reference to the level of education supported by the law as in the following description of grant authorization:

Use of Funds.--Grants awarded under subsection (a) may be used for establishing a technology careers training program to train prisoners for technology-based jobs and careers during the 3-year period before release from prison, jail, or a juvenile facility.
Control of Internet Access.--An entity that receives a grant under subsection (a) shall restrict access to the Internet by prisoners, as appropriate, to ensure public safety. (Second Chance Act, 2007, p. H13570)

In this provision, the prisoner education grants are targeted specifically toward programs that prepare the inmates for "technology-based jobs and careers," with no mention of higher education. Recognizing that many of these programs are internet based, the legislation requires that the grantee restrict students' access to non-programs related websites.

As previously described, there exists a proviso that the programs' contents be monitored by the Attorney General's office.

> Reports.--Not later than the last day of each fiscal year, an entity that receives a grant under subsection (a) during the preceding fiscal year shall submit to the Attorney General a report that describes and assesses the uses of such grant during the preceding fiscal year. (Second Chance Act, 2007, p. H13570)

In another section of the Act, it stipulates that prisoner education programs funded by the federal grants must have their curricula pre-approved by the Justice Department.

In addition to the grants for new programs, the legislation calls for an assessment of existing programs to determine their impact on recidivism. Advocates of prisoner education have often had their claims called in to question due to the lack of comprehensive, national data:

> At the end of each fiscal year, the Director shall submit to the Committee on the Judiciary of the Senate and the Committee on the Judiciary of the House of Representatives a report containing statistics demonstrating the relative reduction in recidivism for inmates released by the Bureau of Prisons within that fiscal year and the 2 prior fiscal years, comparing inmates who participated in major inmate programs (including residential drug treatment, vocational training, and prison industries) with inmates who did not participate in such programs. Such statistics shall be compiled separately for each such fiscal year. (Second Chance Act, 2007, p. H13573)

Inclusion of the provision could be viewed as a victory for the proponents of prisoner education for it will allow the comparison and promotion of the strategies that appear to work. However, there are a couple of weaknesses in the provision: One is that it appears to privilege recidivism reduction as the sole criteria for a positive outcome. First, the studies should take into account a variety of factors, including the prisoner's income, benefits, job satisfaction, degree of involvement in the community and other factors that may affect the well-being of the former inmate as well as society as a whole. The degree to which these issues play out in the lives of the women and men as they leave prison may affect their ability to avoid the criminal justice system in the long-term as well as their ability to positively influence others in their community. For example, a former prisoner who becomes a community activist, counselor, educator or union leader could help others in the sphere of influence to avoid the decisions leading to incarceration much better than someone who has no experience in the penal system. Yet, within the boundaries set by the assessment criteria for re-entry success, their potential contributions to their communities are downplayed in an effort to narrow the criteria to statistically-friendly recidivism rates.

A move to broaden the research methodology beyond quantitative strategies to more inclusive methods within qualitative studies would be a first step toward capturing the wide range of experiences of the former prisoner. A broad-based form of research, combined with the quantitative data would provide a more realistic picture of the relative effectiveness of various pedagogical strategies in integrating ex-inmates back into their communities as full participants. Unfortunately, the language of the bill appears to privilege the scientific method, given that it requires those prisoners who participate in the programs (the experimental group) be compared to those who do not (the control group).

Use of a narrow, positivist method of program evaluation has its cheerleaders, particularly among conservatives. David Muhlhausen of the right-wing Heritage Foundation, testified during the 2010 Senate hearings leading up to reauthorization of the Second Chance Act. He provided a full-throttle defense of the scientific method:

Congress needs to expressly mandate in the reauthorization of the Act the experimental evaluation of prisoner reentry programs. By experimental evaluation, I mean evaluation that uses random assignment to select individuals for treatment and for other individuals to go into control groups. This method is considered the gold standard, because random assignment is most likely to yield valid estimates of program impact. Less rigorous designs yield less reliable results. (p. 10)

The scientific method certainly has its place in knowledge production, especially in the hard sciences such as chemistry and engineering. However, its place in the social sciences is less preeminent. Critics, such as Joe Kincheloe (2008) have suggested that a positivist approach can serve to "undermine the world's appreciation of the complexity of everyday life (p.136)." In addition, by utilizing claims of lack of rigor, positivists, such as Muhlhausen seek to invalidate knowledge that is not situated in their very narrow view of reality. Again according to Kincheloe, "they have constructed a reductionist tap that, like a spigot regulates the mode of data allowed claim standing as verified knowledge" (p. 136). The complexity of the barriers that prisoners face in trying to reenter society and the likely intricacy of the pathways that must be negotiated to successfully take that path cannot be honestly narrowed down to a handful of variables in an experiment. Inmate attitudes, interests and passions are frequently discounted in positivist studies. These should not be variables to be "controlled" in a study, for they are at the very heart of the issue of successful prisoner re-entry. They can be thoroughly examined only through non-positivist, qualitative studies. These attributes may play an important role in determining re-entry outcomes (LeBel, 2009).

The text of the legislation also appears to favor specific kinds of programs by limiting the focus of the research to what it terms "major" programs which it suggests include "drug treatment, vocational training, and prison industries." While these suggestions may not be exclusive, they certainly privilege certain kinds of activities. The message seems clear: If your program does not fall within these categories, it may be suspect and not suitable subject matter for the Bureau of Prison's report and consequently will be denied a means to access the halls of power (the congressional judiciary committees), as well as funding. While the described study itself may serve to provide a voice to certain truths regarding the relative effectiveness of the various kinds of programs designed to reduce recidivism, there exists an institutional bias in both the kinds of programs privileged by language and in the ones that are considered for actual funding. The distinction is important, for there are some innovative prisoner education programs (cited later in this work) that are run by volunteers; or receive funding from non-federal sources that, although small in scope, could offer valuable information regarding the possibilities for enhancing or facilitating prisoner re-entry. These programs would probably be excluded from the federal study by not meeting the criterion of being "major" or fitting into the narrow, vocationalized view of what constitutes valid prisoner education.

With the range of educational options sharply narrowed to vocational/technical and job training, there would be an accompanying limitation on the kinds of occupations open to the former inmates. Several representatives addressed this issue in the course of the debates. Representative Tubbs-Jones, in one passage, mentions a re-entry program where: "We did a painting business with ex-offenders and a catering business with ex-offenders" (Second Chance Hearing, 2005, p. 51). In her story of Derrick, the young man climbed the ladder of success when he obtained employment at a Wendy's Restaurant followed by a job in construction. The commonality of these areas of employment is that they are all in the service and trade sectors. While certainly worthwhile occupations, they by no means span the breadth of employment possibilities for those who are not former prisoners. There is no mention of "professional" lines of work such as nurses, engineers and teachers, all of which are experiencing acute shortages in many sections of the country. Nor are other professions listed: accountant or architect. These are all fields that require extensive study through a dedicated, time intensive effort. Time is one commodity in great abundance in prison. As previously mentioned, over half of the women and men in prison in America have a high school diploma or the equivalent and are considered qualified to take college courses. Yet, within the confines of the worldview of the writers of the Second Chance Act, they are suitable only for training in technical or service industry positions. Many prisoners may choose this path and should be given the opportunity. But for those who would endeavor to enter other professions, they should also be given a chance. This could be an opportunity they did not receive before - considering most prisoners are people of color and/or from low-income communities. It could be a chance for educational access denied from the beginning given the economic, racial and other societal barriers for those coming from such a background. It may be too early to give them a second opportunity, for they may not have received their first chance.

Summary of the Debates

Several debate passages from the early 1990s, cited in the previous chapter, had all the features of moral panic. Common traits included identification of crime as a threat requiring immediate action, and of society's fundamental values at risk. Opponents to prisoner Pell Grants had little ideological commonality. They included liberals and conservatives. In analyzing their rhetoric, the focal argument was a strategy to marginalize prisoners through discursive efforts. Their attempts centered on a syntactic construction of those studying inside prison as exclusively "prisoners," "inmates," and "convicts." These they juxtaposed against "legitimate," law-abiding Pell grantees who were "men and women," "students," "children," and "citizens," a bit of world building that essentializes prisoners as the Other separate from Us.

The Pell Grant opponents further engaged in myth-making by repeating a "true story" of a police officer whose child was denied a Pell Grant because prisoners were eligible. On examination, it appeared the officer's income was too high to qualify for the grant. That detail did not inhibit the retelling of the tale by several Pell Grant opponents as they attempted to re-enforce a societal binary.

Those in favor of Pell Grants for prisoners tended to have greater ideological homogeneity, consisting primarily of old-line white liberals, such as Claiborne Pell and members of the progressive Congressional Black Caucus. Senator Pell tried to defend prisoner Pell Grants through authority arguments involving recidivism rates data. He also sought to problematize the Us/Them polarity through inclusive language and by pointing out that one of his debate opponents had a felony indictment.

Members of the Congressional Black Caucus also used recidivism data. However, their argument was essentially economic using a cost/benefit analysis of prisoner education. They attempted to construct prisoners as potential human capital for industry.

Those members of Congress who spoke in opposition of the Second Chance Act appear to be ideologically pure as a group, coming from the right wing of the Republican Party. They, like the Pell Grant opponents, attempted to marginalize prisoners as the Other.

Proponents of the Second Chance Act are somewhat ideologically diverse, including conservatives. This may reflect President Bush's support. Proponents take on several discursive strategies. They include authority arguments involving recidivism rates and cost/benefit analysis of prisoner education. The Second Chance Act debate, perhaps due to a major faith-based initiative component of the legislation, has much more religious-themed rhetoric, virtually absent in the Pell Grant transcripts. Finally, a commonality of the prisoner Pell Grant and Second Chance debates is the focus on education exclusively as a means of reconstructing prisoners as human capital. This has strong implications for the construction of the Act, particularly the provisions regarding prisoner education which are geared almost entirely toward basic education and job training.

There is a relationship of these findings to issues of the role of rhetoric and policy in the construction of identity of Others and the creation and maintenance of social dominance. This relationship will be examined in the next chapter along with an alternative way of envisioning pedagogy in prisons.

CHAPTER 7

Insights and Implications

The analysis of the debates over prisoner education reveals myriad strategies utilized in order to win over support for the various standpoints of the stakeholders. These perspectives comprise a broad ideological spectrum. They include the view that prisoners are victims of an unjust criminal system, that they made "bad decisions" and can be "rehabilitated" by remolding themselves into productive features of the labor market. In addition, there was the standpoint, particularly prevalent during the Pell Grant debates, that the women and men who committed felonies were unredeemable and should be banished permanently to the margins of society. Each of these viewpoints has important implications for the kinds of policies they engender, ranging from the desiccation of the Pell Grant funding to the creation of the Second Chance Act education programs emphasizing vocationalism. In this section, I will attempt to reveal how these frameworks of understanding can relate to the strategies of maintenance and/or accentuation of social dominance within the larger narratives of power relations in society. Debate discourse served to "sell" the above mentioned myths in order to enhance and accentuate hierarchies. The policies resulting from the debates, many embedded in the philosophy of neoliberalism also have a role in the maintenance of social strata.

A frequent narrative within the Pell Grant debates is that of the moral panic as elucidated by Specter and Dornan. Critical to each debater's argument is the supposition that the peril originates from without (from the Other) and within (through corruption of Us). Both suggest the crime wave is a result of moral laxity, which has the potential to further corrupt our nation's youth by "fostering a permanent urban underclass living outside the common values of our society." The panic comes from both the immorality of the Other, manifest in the crime wave, and the potential to corrupt Our morals. Barriers are said to be needed to shield the law-abiding, well-to-do groups. This separation is accomplished by the means I will describe below.

One strategy is the physical walls of the prisons themselves. Over 2.3 million women and men are separated from the rest of society through this means. This was the strategy most advocated at the time of the 1994 Crime Bill debates that resulted in the massive prison build up over the next decade. Since the dominant approach to crime was an attitude of "lock-'em-up and to hell with the consequences," educating prisoners was seen as a waste of funding. Opponents of prisoner Pell Grants sought legitimacy for this strategy through discourse to portray criminals as Them who they put into conflict with Us at every turn. This oppositional approach became part of the Pell Grant debates through the efforts of conservatives and liberals alike. Micro-analysis of the debate talk reveals many instances of discursive efforts to create archetypical "victims" of prisoner's use of Pell Grants. These archetypes included children of police officers who were supposedly denied Pell funding for college due to the overreaching of the inmate students. Within this moral tale, the protagonist (police officer) is tempted to cross over to the Other Side by breaking the law to secure money for his children's college. Instead, the good officer turns to a Higher Power (the Congressman) to tell his story and receive help. This moral tale was repeated several times in the Pell Grant debates. The finding was not exclusive to this study. In his 2004 examination of the debates over the 1994 Crime Bill, Joshua Page found similar results. By acting as the ultimate arbiters of the injustices perpetuated on Us by Them, the representatives "portrayed themselves as Robin Hoods who took from the non-deserving prisoners and give to the deserving, disadvantaged students" in what Page termed a "penal drama" with heroes and villains (p. 373).

Despite the gallant efforts of a few progressive legislators, such as the Congressional Black Caucus, severe criminal penalties, funding for a massive prison build-up and a denial of the main source of prisoner education funding-grants were codified within the 1994 Crime Bill.

The moral panic fostered by the media and politicians such as Dornan and Specter had as its result massive incarceration and a diminution of prisoner education. However, arguments in favor of massive incarceration began to lose currency in the early 2000s. As previously related, America's position as the world's chief incarcerator led to questions regarding the legitimacy of a political and economic system that resulted in the mass imprisonment of its underclass. These concerns reached their apex in communities hardest hit, such as those represented by the Congressional Black Caucus. Equally prominent were the fiscal concerns, outlined earlier, at the federal and state levels relative to the building and maintenance of a vast prison system. These two concerns: de-legitimization of the prison state and budgetary costs provided a pressure that moved politicians to seek an alternative to massive incarceration. However, key to the acceptability of this alternative was its ability to meet the often competing interests and ideologies of the stakeholders. An acceptable alternative was found in the educational and other re-entry policies embedded within the Second Chance Act.

The ideological diversity of the proponents of the Second Chance Act stood in stark contrast to the standpoints of the opponents. Advocates of the legislation ranged from far-right Reagan-school conservatives to the more progressive New Deal-style liberals and the members of the Black Caucus. Opponents of the re-entry program positioned themselves to the right of their Republican congressional leaders and President Bush. In many ways these paleoconservatives utilized debate tactics that harkened back to those opposed to the prisoner Pell Grants by situating themselves as Us versus the inmates (Them). You were either against Us or against Them with little room for moral ambiguity. More than likely it is not a coincidence that Carter and Gohmert, the two primary advocates of this extreme frontier justice, hailed from Texas. It was there that they built their political reputations as tough-on-crime trial judges (Congressional Quarterly, 2005, p.971). Having solidified their political reputations primarily on a position of demonizing both prisoners and those who coddle them, it may have been difficult for them to conduct an apparent about face by supporting the Second Chance Act. Consequently, they continued the tried and true tactics dictated by their narrow ideological standpoint by attempting to further marginalize those convicted of crimes. In their world prisoners are in binary opposition to "average American citizens." Interestingly, they continue the rhetorical tactics of the Pell opponents by constructing a story involving a model citizen who is denied government funding due to the greed of grant-seeking inmates. Unlike the Pell debates where the story's protagonist was a police officer, Gohmert et al updated the tale to reflect America's wartime footing and the hero becomes an ex-serviceman. Like the pilgrim in the previous tale, the serviceman also faces the moral decision to turn to crime as a means to secure the needed funds only to be "saved" by the intervention of his defender who happens to be the congressman. In the Pell debates these tactics appeared to have worked and Pell was denied prisoners by an overwhelming vote.

By the early 2000s, prisoner education opponents such as Gohmert and Carter were faced with opposition from both the rival party and their own leaders. However, given their investment in a very narrow, specific narrative regarding prisoners as the Other, they continued their rhetorical efforts on the House floor. They may have noted Newt Gingrich labored in relative obscurity for years, gathering a C-SPAN-nursed hardcore following by advocating policies to the right of his party's leadership before bursting onto the scene to a position of power when the time was ripe.

Gohmert and company were in the small minority of the representatives who voted against the Second Chance Act. However, they were not ideologically isolated. Many of the Act's Republican advocates, such as Coble, Cannon, and Brownback held voting records as conservative as those who opposed the legislation. The party line included support for limited government spending, particularly when it involved social service programs. So why would the Second Chance Act attract the votes of these die-hard fiscal conservatives? After all, the Act entailed creation of a government program projected to spend $300 million over two years on a group of people who a decade earlier had been vilified and confined through the 1994 Crime Bill (O'Hear, 2007). Many aspects of the Second Chance Act appeared to typify the kinds of programs conservatives railed against for years, such as government sponsored prisoner education, counseling, healthcare and job placement. What was it about the bill that not only drew their support, but their outspoken advocacy? As the saying goes, the devil is in the details.

The Second Chance Act provides a commitment for a new federal role in re-entry through dedicated funding for a variety of re-entry services, including education. In many ways the Act represents a new way of seeing prisoners and their needs on a holistic level, but was this vision adequately backed up with the dollars? Is this another highly publicized, but under-funded mandate? The math appears to support the latter view, with the total funding authorized by the Act coming to an average of about $225 for each of the estimated number of prisoners to be released over the following two years. The Second Chance Act, however, is not solely a function of its budget. There are aspects of the legislation that extend far beyond its funding allocations. They include its commitment to public-private partnerships, particularly faith-based initiatives, and the Act's disciplining effect on its participants in the form of its strict treatment of them as human capital in the free market. In addition, inclusion of formerly non-carceral welfare initiatives, such as the nominal transitional housing, healthcare and employment services within the context of the criminal justice system, serves to highlight the "legitimacy" of the legislation as a means to control by "helping." In the next sections of this chapter, I will discuss these three features of the Act, including the rhetorical devices utilized in the debates to provide legitimacy to their inclusion in the bill and their implications for prisoner education.

Faith-based Initiatives

The Second Chance Act's provisions direct funding for religious organizations to provide mentoring and other re-entry services for newly released prisoners. Perhaps due to its inclusion in the Act's provisions, references to religion became much more prominent in the Second Chance debates than was seen in the discourse over the Pell Grant for prisoners. The references in the Second Chance talk appeared to reflect both the speakers' views of spirituality and how they justify a political standpoint through religious beliefs. The example from Representative Gohmert indicated his opposition to the Second Chance re-entry program arose, at least in part from his interpretation of the New Testament text. He suggested that government's role should be restricted to a punitive function and that social services were the domain of individuals. His statement came in response to Tubbs-Jones' speech citing the same scripture, only her interpretation was that the state has a role in helping prisoners. In many ways their dialogue reflects a fundamental divide between a Left interpretation of what has been termed "social gospel" and a Right interpretation.

The social gospel is the belief that religious institutions have a role in society that extends beyond the walls of the temple or church. This responsibility is manifest in various forms of civic engagement ranging from advocating for or against issues such as abortion, school prayer, and the death penalty to lobbying for legislation or even supporting specific candidates. Conservative, fundamentalist Christians who tend to adhere to a "strict interpretation" of their bible are often anti-abortion and pro-school prayer and death penalty. They include the Christian Coalition and Family Research Council. Less conservative religions tend to take a more nuanced view of these issues (Weigel, 1996). They include the Church of Christ, Methodist Church and Reform Jews. All of the five organizations named above were attracted to the Second Chance Act and lent their names as formal endorsers. So, while Gohmert represented one conservative Christian interpretation of their bible, other conservative Christian representatives, such as Chris Cannon, had a different view. In the aforementioned excerpts, Cannon makes clear his opinion that America should adhere to one set of values, Christian-based. However, unlike Gohmert, Cannon finds these values embedded in the Second Chance Act. The faith-based mentoring provisions may have drawn his support. As mentioned before, Cannon's attitude towards immigrants was shaped in part through his experiences as a missionary in South America. Perhaps the legislation's support of mentoring programs facilitated by religious organizations appealed to his missionary zeal.

Tubbs-Jones was not the only Congressperson to approach a social gospel from the Left. Danny Davis made numerous religious references in the course of the prisoner education and re-entry debates as did other members of the Congressional Black Caucus. The white, liberal supporters of the Act appeared to utilize little religious rhetoric in their debate speech. So why were the members of the Black Caucus more effusive in their use of religious references? The answer may lie in the special place the Black Church has had in the Black struggle for justice and freedom.

In his autobiography, U.S. Congressman John Lewis (1998) narrates the vital role played by religious faith and the institution of the

Black Church in the Civil Rights movement. With his experiences with seminal movement events such as the early sit-ins, boycotts, right up to the March on Washington, the church provided both a logistical base for organizational events and a spiritual base for ideological justification through interpretation of scripture. According to Lewis, the civil rights workers were often sustained in troubling times through uplifting gospel songs or the powerful voices of the ministers who served as leaders. No movement leader typified this influence more than Dr. Martin Luther King, Jr. In the following excerpt from his book, Congressman Lewis describes the first time he heard Dr. King:

> On a Sunday morning in early 1955, I was listening to our radio, tuned to WRMA out of Montgomery, as always, when on the air came a sermon by a voice I'd never heard before a young minister from Atlanta... I listened, as this man spoke about how it wasn't enough for black people to be concerned only with getting to the Promised Land in the hereafter, about how it was not enough for people to be concerned with roads that are paved with gold, and gates to the Kingdom of God. He said we needed to be concerned with the gates of schools that are closed to black people and the doors of stores that refused to hire or serve us. His message was one of love and the Gospel, but he was applying to *now* (emphasis his). (p. 45)

The church's influence on the Black struggle in the U.S. predates the 1950s and has roots in the ways "African-American slaves appropriated and reworked Christian faith in the context of their experience of slavery" (Antonio, 2007, p. 79).

Given the place of Christianity in the lived culture of the Black struggle, it should come as no surprise that religious wording would be prominent in the speech of the Black Caucus members regarding the Second Chance Act. Even though members of the Black Caucus were also involved in the prisoner Pell Grant debates, there is a paucity of religious rhetoric in their speech of the time. There are several possible reasons for the difference. One might be the individuals themselves. A few Black Caucus members were involved in both debates. The primary figures in the Pell debates were Wynn, Conyers, Towns,

Owens, and Mfume. Conyers, Davis, Tubbs-Jones, and Jackson-Lee were the key Black Caucus figures in the Second Chance debates. Only Conyers took a prominent role in both debates. Different people have their own rhetorical styles. Another possible difference may have been an institutional bias away from religious references. Congressional debate is one step away from Congressional action which is codified in legislative language that is usually devoid of religious reference due to constitutional restraints. This may place an inhibiting effect on religious talk. This bias, however, was as likely to apply in the early 2000s as it would a decade before. There were other aspects of the debates that were different that may have had a modifying influence on the bias. One was the leadership of the Black Caucus in the Second Chance Act debate, relative to that of the Pell debates. By the time of the Act's debates, John Conyers had become chairman of the House Judiciary Committee. Consequently, he was able to exert a great deal of influence over both the nature of the Second Chance Act legislation and also the proceedings surrounding its enactment. Committee hearings would be set up that prominently featured Black Caucus supporters. In this collegial environment, members may have felt more comfortable in using "informal" language that included religious references in the Act's debates. Finally, with its provisions for faith-based rhetoric, the nature of the Second Chance Act itself may have influenced the speakers. Beyond the legislative specifics, the overall goals of the Act may have had an impact. When Sheila Jackson-Lee, describing the legislation, suggests that prisoners can be "redeemed by the grace of a second chance," the spiritual connotations are clear. This is language not found in the Pell Grant debates.

One question that arises is how two seemingly disparate traditions, black social gospel and white, conservative fundamentalism, could so easily find common ground in the Second Chance Act. As with many pieces of omnibus legislation, supporters often voted for legislation that contained seemingly odious provisions in the interest of having other aspects become law. One apropos example was the time a few members of the Black Caucus supported the 1994 Crime Bill. Even though amendments to the bill broadened application of the death penalty, which they opposed, the overall legislation also contained funding for drug treatment and domestic abuse provisions they favored.

It is unlikely that a broad, diverse coalition such as the one that gathered around the Second Chance Act would find its constituents unanimously in favor of all of the bill's parts. Much of the ideological back and forth over the legislative provisions may have taken place in the committees where the real work of putting together bills occurs. By the time the legislation has been voted out of committee compromises have been made. Then committee members concentrate on obtaining support on the floor from their fellow legislators for their "win-win" bill, and are less likely to speak ill of it. Supporters are not going to highlight, on C-SPAN, the aspects of legislation they find abhorrent and that they will ultimately vote into law.

For the most part, clues to their preferences are likely to be found in their past legislative voting records, or by sifting through the debate speech of the bill's advocates to reveal a few points of contention. Chris Cannon dropped one statement into his speech that probably has import for understanding Second Chance's inclusion and promotion of the public-private partnerships, including faith-centered initiatives. As recounted earlier, he said: "You don't have to believe in God to be an American, but most Americans, believers or not, when given a choice will support limiting government to promote the welfare of their fellow man. For believers like me, this legislation does that." Within the context of their opposition to state-sponsored social programs, conservative support for the Second Chance Act makes perfect sense if seen as one means to shift responsibility for welfare from the government to private concerns. As Wineburg pointed out earlier in his critique of faith-based initiatives, the policy should be viewed in context of an "individualistic message" of social service. This project serves to move welfare out of the collective domain toward that of the private entities, each with their individual agendas. David Harvey (2005) has pointed out that neoliberal philosophy embraces public-private partnerships as a means to shift government responsibilities to the private sector. These partnerships often serve as a way to allow private entities to influence regulatory activities of Congress as well as participation in drafting legislation. They had greater access in an environment of downsized government which appeared to be ideal for participation by faith-based organizations. Ethan Sharp (2010) noted that Bush's Office of Faith Based and Community Initiatives "emerged amid diminishing opportunities for the federal government to reinforce and expand social programs because of the ascendency of neoliberalism" (p.55). Religious organizations that endorsed the legislation, such as the Christian Coalition and the Family Research Council, are provided an opportunity to influence the direction of legislative provisions, possibly setting up a role in the bill's enactment by receiving grants for re-entry services. Within light of this proposition, conservative support and promotion of a large social program for prisoners is not surprising. By potentially increasing their influence on the legislation; as well as privatizing government services, conservatives had much to gain.

Formatted Lives

This discussion began with a description of the need for an alternative to massive incarceration. The need arose due to both the rising costs of high incarceration rates and incarceration's decreasing legitimacy as the sole means to control crime in the eyes of many of our nation's stakeholders. Due to their relatively low costs, the prisoner education and other reentry programs of the Second Chance Act meet the first requirement. The Act's various components such as faith-centered initiatives and other public-private aspects and mentoring by religious groups appeal to some constituencies. The focus on reducing recidivism through education and other programs is attractive to others and there is probably enough crossover support to legitimize the project in the eyes of many. A central part of this legitimization process was the use of the debates to highlight and gain support both from within the Congressional chambers and from without through C-SPAN. A key device in the debates was the selective highlighting of portions of the legislation that was palatable to each legislator's targeted constituency. Conservatives coated their piece of the pie in rhetoric geared for their target audience and progressives did the same. Thus, the representatives were able to craft a seemingly win-win situation in the eyes of all (or at least the most influential) stakeholders.

There is one aspect of the Second Chance Act that I have yet to discuss. If, as earlier suggested, the primary reason for massive incarceration is to control communities that have undergone marginalization due to economic policies, how does the Second Chance Act achieve this end? What is the role of the debate rhetoric in providing legitimacy to activities that maintain this social separation? In light of the data I will seek to address these questions.

As previously described, a major tenet of neoliberal philosophy is the re-positioning of welfare from the non-carceral domain into that of the criminal justice system. For the roughly 2.3 million prisoners; housing, medical care, education and employment are provided within the walls of prison. But what about the 5.2 million ex-inmates who are on probation or parole? The Second Chance Act represents a first major step by the federal government toward integrating the formerly non-penal welfare services into the criminal justice system through the establishment of transitional housing, medical care and other services. However, the legislation extends far beyond the regulatory aspects described by Piven and Cloward (1983), of traditional welfare, reinforcing the perception of prisoner re-entry as a "totalizing" project. The Second Chance Act contains several mechanisms of formal control including re-entry courts where judges are delegated solely to the task of monitoring each person's transition back into the community. The courts would work in tandem with law enforcement and community organizations, and keep track of the ex-prisoners' progress in education, job training, drug counseling, and other re-entry requirements. Michael O'Hear (2007), of Marquette University's law school suggests the establishment of these courts while ostensibly touted as a means to facilitate a smooth transition, can serve to accentuate recidivism. Having judges administer re-entry programs,
"may lead to neglect of the full human potential of returnees, as well as a tendency to pull the 're-exit' trigger too quickly for the returnees who appear to present the highest risk of re-offense" (p.11).

O'Hear is not alone in raising concerns regarding the re-entry courts. Maruna and LeBel (2010) suggest many re-entry courts are based upon a "control narrative" which applies the same kind of punishment orientation toward those who are released as those who are still in prison. Even courts that utilize a mixed rewards/punishment model are flawed. It is assumed that prisoners will become self-motivated to succeed when placed within a re-entry system that attempts to "program" good behavior with a simplistic carrot/stick approach.

In addition to controlling the recently released by its statutes, there are several glaring omissions from the Act's re-entry provisions. The convicted felon, once released, faces a lifetime of limitations due to her or his criminal record. These range from denial of employment, to banning from public housing to restrictions on student aid. Many states ban felons from a host of licensures ranging from cosmetology to educators. Congress could have limited these strictures to a narrow list of appropriately sensitive occupations such as banning drug offenders from working in pharmacies, but did not. The Act could have limited access to criminal records to a need-to-know basis. In addition, the legislation could have overridden the myriad state laws restricting or even banning those convicted of a felony from voting. These glaring omissions leave former prisoners open to a life of restrictions and regulations governing just about every part of their lives from where they live to where they work and go to school, and even including basic rights such as the ability to vote or run for public office. These are what Representative Davis so aptly called the "invisible punishments."

There were also informal methods of control embedded in the prisoner education debates. With the narrative of Us vs. Them, the representatives situated themselves as defenders of the status quo. This strategy is probably as old as politics itself. In light of the data and analysis from this study, Joshua Page's characterization of the Pell Grant debates as a penal drama designed to garner electoral support for the various parties appears entirely plausible. Yet, the denial of the Pell Grant became a key link in a chain of events leading to a much more complex form of world building, one that somewhat blurs the designation of Other within the discourse of a more subtle level. Removing Pell Grant access from the students in prison helped to establish the framework of conditions leading to this new method of control, for it was the void left by the elimination of the Pell Grant that was partially filled by the establishment of the Second Chance Act education programs.

The Pell-sponsored education programs, which could range from vocational to liberal arts, provided the students with a degree of agency in that they had the potential to choose what level or kind of education was offered. As will be described later, prisoner students could initiate and help establish educational programs that were relatively autonomous to the institutions where they were housed. Because the student often has some control over where she wants to apply her grant, there is a certain level of academic freedom that seems to be almost entirely absent in the Second Chance Act education programs.

The government's control over the programs appears to be complete at almost every level of the educational process in the Second Chance Act, including establishment of goals, application of funding, curricular development, as well as the assessment of outcomes. Education is clearly situated as a controlled-access system. By shunting prisoners through job training programs and adult education, the policy does not take into account pre-existing credentials. Most prisoners possess a GED or high school diploma and are technically qualified for college-level courses - opportunities denied in the Act's provisions. Moving beyond credentialization, the legislation's provisions focus on assessing "needs and deficits" without taking into account both formal education and the informal learning that took place in prior work experiences. Regarding talents and positive attributes, the Second Chance Act apparently assumes and privileges a view of prisoner as a *tabla rasa* to be remodeled into an ideal worker. What does this ideal entail? Answers may be found by looking at the debate data.

Several of the Congress members, in advocating for the Second Chance Act, cited its potential to remold prisoners into "productive" beings. Within the context of the speeches, productive is defined as holding a job, paying taxes, and obeying the law. Productivity outside of these three domains is rarely mentioned. There were a few references to civic engagement, but only within the confines of voting. The men and women were not seen as having a future as artists, organizers, or politicians. Nor were they imagined outside low-income occupations. Yet they were expected to lead fulfilled lives, laboring in obscurity at their low-wage jobs. Examples of model citizens were given whose chief attributes appear to have been the ability to stay out of trouble, show up to work on time and not piss off the boss. Thus, the policy appears to mold these women and men into suitable bodies for the market.

The Second Chance Act provides several means of maintaining these women and men within this model of existence. One is formal education involving job training and basic education. Besides the limitations of the resulting credentials, confining prisoners within this framework of learning sends a message to them (and others) that they have less capability than Us. This message can function as a self-fulfilling prophecy.

Another possible means of control is the faith-based mentoring. Having religious institutions provide mentors to the prisoners or recently released men and women is problematic on several levels including Constitutional issues, and respect for religious preference or lack of preference. In addition, it would be impossible to monitor the occurrence and/or degree of proselytizing. This potential is particularly troubling given the subordinate position in which the prisoner would be placed relative to a court appointed mentor. Even under the best of circumstances where the mentor seeks to respect the mentee's spiritual choices, the mentor still has a task involving transmission of values through a personal relationship. This relationship could be built upon the ex-inmate trusting the mentor to provide him or her with guidance on a broad range of life choices, extending far beyond whether or not to break the law. Thus, the mentor would have an inordinate amount of influence over the one who is mentored. The mentor would pass along values from whatever her perspective may be. Given the broad, ideological range of religious organizations sponsoring Second Chance, these values are likely to be wide ranging, at least within the Judeo-Christian framework. However, there apparently were no Muslim, Hindu, Quaker, Buddhist or any other minority religious organizations among the Act's endorsers.

In the years since the passage of the Second Chance Act and its outsourcing of many re-entry services to nonprofit organizations there has been an emphasis on Christian-based groups. According to prison educator Megan Sweeney (2010):

> In prisons throughout the country, the increase in state and federal funding rehabilitative programming has been matched by an increase in the presence of Christian volunteers, reading materials and educational programs... This influx has meant that some opportunities, privileges and reading materials are available only to prisoners who are willing to embrace a Christian perspective. (P. 174)

Since the time the Second Chance Act was enacted, the federal government has not only provided tacit approval, but in some cases open support to Christian-based prisoner education groups. An example would be the Seeds of Hope Jail Ministry which was created to "spread worship to inmates." In 2010 it received $298,849 in Second Chance Act funding from the U.S. Justice Department to set up a mentoring program in conjunction with the Catholic Social Services and the Salvation Army (Gray, 2010 p.1).

A mentoring initiative, as an aspect of the prisoner's education, is troubling. Not the least problematic is the potential for abuse on many levels by these non-government employees. What will be their qualifications, training, or certifications? Who will monitor their interactions? Will men "mentor" only men and women only counsel with women? Children who are under probation have been known to experience sexual abuse from their probation officers (Ferro, 2011). Having non-governmental workers mentoring these young girls and boys takes away a layer of accountability. Who regulates the interactions with youth offenders to prevent abuse? These questions obtain greater urgency in the situations when the "unofficial" faith-based mentors have the coercive force of law behind them.

Despite all of the above-mentioned open questions regarding the faith-based mentoring initiative, there is one certainty – it will serve as a means to discipline the post-release participants. Mentoring serves as a means of values transmission. While the Act does not stipulate exactly what these values will entail, they are likely to represent a Judeo-Christian outlook with emphasis on obedience and hard work. Representative Tubbs-Jones (2005) makes just such an inference when she described a re-entry program she helped found: "In the community program that is run by Lutheran Metropolitan Ministries, our motto is that people are more likely to act their way into a new way of thinking than think their way into a new way of acting" (p. H11095). This slogan represents a puritan view of work that values action before thought, i.e., do not question, do and your answers will come to you.

Under the guise of helping prisoners ease back into the free world, the Second Chance Act appears to be a totalizing project designed to regulate every aspect of an ex-inmate's life. It appears to fulfill the three primary needs of a palatable alternative to massive imprisonment. Firstly, it attempts to reduce the financial costs associated with warehousing inmates. This is accomplished, in part by following a neoliberal strategy of shifting a portion of responsibility for re-entry services to non-profits. Secondly, it attempts to legitimize penal policy by establishing a host of re-entry programs including education, job training and other support services. The policies proved attractive to some stakeholders while others were drawn to the Act's establishment of public-private partnerships. Congressional rhetoric reflected the ideological standpoints of the participants who emphasized aspects of the legislation that appealed to their constituents. Ultimately, the Second Chance Act appears to function as a means to retain control of marginalized groups even as they are allowed back into free society. Control is maintained through re-entry courts and other legal structures that serve to leave wide open the door of recidivism. Faith-based mentoring programs are a means to enhance or establish hegemony through the indoctrination of "common sense" values that can serve to disguise political or religious ideology. Diminution of agency is achieved by restricting prisoner's educational access to narrow, vocationalized choices. Restriction of educational opportunity to basic adult education and job training further marginalizes men and women who are released from prison. This hampers their potential to compete with those who, by virtue of access to higher education, are at the top of the job market.

In his critique of the criminalization aspects of neoliberal governing, Wacquant (2008) suggests the goal of keeping workers within the confines of the criminal justice system is to provide further advantage to the business class. These gains are maintained by providing un-secure, low-wage jobs with few benefits for the poor and through the establishment of a justice system that serves as a *de facto* ghetto. By narrowly defining post-incarceration "freedom," the Second Chance Act serves this goal by fortifying rather than diminishing the hierarchies in society.

The Second Chance Act establishes a disciplinary regime that appears to limit the potential for ex-inmates to take control of their own destinies. It is possible that some of the harder edges of the legislation may be softened upon implementation. The law calls for the Justice Department's approval of educational projects funded by the Act. Which president occupies the White House could affect the outcome of this approval process. The Obama Administration has indicated willingness to attempt to maintain separation of Church and State (Bauer and Chivakos, 2010). In addition, the kinds of faith-based organizations receiving funding for transitional services could be affected. These kinds of changes in the presidential attitudes may privilege mainstream religious organizations over fundamentalist church groups that are more likely to proselytize. However, it is important to understand that these possibilities are driven by factors exogenous to the will of the former inmates. The core concept of the policy remains centered around the idea of ex-prisoners without the ability to have significant freedom to shape their own destinies.

Emancipatory Education

Education can serve as one means of emancipation by providing tools to help former inmates build the knowledge and motivation that comes with the ability to make free choices. This capacity or agency is critical to successful re-entry. It is this potential that I will propose as one alternative to the Second Chance Act's narrow, deterministic vision of life for the formerly incarcerated women and men. There is an alternative that seeks to recognize the centrality of agency in their journey to freedom.

In the 1970s and 1980s, a trend arose in prisoner education in which prisoners were viewed as active participants in their own learning (Bernstein, 2010). It was the inmates themselves who were often at the forefront of initiating a new prison pedagogy that was highly critical of both the criminal justice system as well as the wider social and economic institutions that gave rise to the inequities that constituted the police/penal state. Within this school of thought, prisons are seen as an integral part of a politico/economic system that survives, as Germanotta, (1995) suggests, by "maintaining unequal relations at the level of production. Penal institutions are the ultimate vehicle used to police the borderlines of these unequal relations." It should not come as a surprise that inmates are often at the forefront of the push for a critical prison pedagogy since, "living and working within [correctional] settings will make this abundantly clear" (p.104).

James Morse (2002), a former prisoner, deftly analyzes the unequal relations manifest in the Harlem, Bedford Stuyvesant, Lower East Side, and South Bronx neighborhoods of New York City.

These urban sectors are not neighborhoods in the traditionally middle-class sense of socially stable, economically viable residential areas. Owing largely to the polarizing effect of conservative economics during the Reagan/ Bush debacle whereby the rich become super-rich and the poor become super-poor - these sectors are principally pockets of extremely low income and dependency, exhibiting a constant and rapid turnover of residents that establishes social instability as the prevailing norm. Promoting this social instability, and characterizing these enclaves as prisoner specific, is the perpetual outflow and influx of myriads of individuals to and from the state's prison system. (p. 129)

Educators have described some of the many forms that critical prison pedagogy can take: from inmates becoming self-aware and aware of societal ills through the reading, distribution and analysis of literature of the industrial trade unions; Black and Chicano power and other resistance movements; to the influx of volunteer educators in the 1970s inspired by the well-publicized prisoner resistance activities of that period. Other forms of emancipatory education include self-taught inmate "lawyers" who educate their peers on the vagaries of negotiating the legal system or a group of women prisoners who staged a successful protest when their writing workshop was threatened with cancellation (Davidson, 1995). Education of this kind has the potential to help prisoners to become active, involved citizens. Paulo Friere (1970) describes the possibilities of emancipatory education, "people develop their power to perceive critically the way they exist in the world with which and in which they find themselves; they come to see the world not as a static reality, but as a reality in process, in transformation" (p. 83). What better place to facilitate transformational pedagogy than prison? Eggleston and Gehring (2000), longtime prison educators, describe the potential for innovative programs in the penal environment, "Democratic programs in correctional education are compelling to the human spirit – they conjure up ancient aspirations." These aspirations include "freedom" and a "just/democratic society" (p.310).

One means of facilitating emanicipatory education for those incarcerated is by putting into place funding mechanisms that have few curricular strings attached and can allow for innovation. These could give the prisoners themselves some level of autonomy in choosing what kind of education they would receive. Necessary to the establishment of democratic education is reliable non-program specific funding. An example of such a funding mechanism was the Pell Grant program.

Prisons are representative of "total institutions," characterized by authoritarianism and regimentation and close observation of its inhabitants (Goffman, 1961). Thomas James (1988) has suggested that schools can also be totalizing organizations, marked by their ability to cause "dissolution of the self as the corporate identity of the total institution emerges from within and becomes a way of life" (p.2). While authoritarianism provides a common thread between many schools and all prisons, there is one major difference, most schools are day schools, allowing egress on a daily basis. Freedom of movement has the potential to provide access to new ideas through exposure to non-sanctioned media and new associations. Prisons, at least in theory, are set up to strictly regulate both the bodies and the minds of the inmates by controlling whatever passes through the gates. Foucault (1995) suggests that prisons function to create "docile bodies" through continuous observation. Because the gaze tends to be one way, toward the prisoners, they never know when they are being observed. This process tends to discipline the mind as well as the body. The result is to create a compliant person, with a diminution of agency.

Prison life is devoid of the choices most people have the agency to make. Inmates are usually told what to eat, drink, when the lights are turned on and off or even when to use the toilet. They often face restrictions as to when to speak, read, or write. Yet, after living for years under these conditions they are expected to emerge to the outside world and act with agency to resist the many pressures that precipitated their acquiescence to criminal behaviors in the first place. The lack of logic behind current U.S. criminal justice policy is astounding.

Despite the totalizing nature of most prisons, a reading of the prisoner education literature reveals instances where prison administrations have been remarkably open-minded in allowing prisoners access to educational programs whose content has been critical of not only the institutions themselves, but also of the wider political and economic conditions that gave rise to their existence. Some of these programs are grounded in class struggle, others in Latino and Black Liberation, Feminism and other liberation movements. Not all were funded by Pell Grants; however, they will be described to demonstrate *possibility*.

Davidson (1995) advocates a penal pedagogy with roots in critical criminology, where " the conditions that produce most criminal activity are eliminated not by the domestication of individuals, but by their politicalization: by individuals become conscious of themselves as historical beings who demand to create social forms that are conducive to genuine social justice" (p. 11). The nurturing of political consciousness in prisoners had been the goal of several higher education programs of the decade preceding prisoner Pell Grant elimination. Peter Linebaugh (1995) describes his experiences teaching at Massachusetts correctional facilities in the 1970s. He taught using, among other sources, Cloward and Piven and Rousseau. Guest lecturers included a historian, whose specialty was the American labor movement and a Buddhist scholar. Linebaugh pulled no punches when challenging the inmate students with advanced material and his students responded in kind, translating the concepts into their languages. "Cynicism was widespread. Some of it was wide awake, such as 'To kill the Indians they hire Irish who're starving because of the potato famine'" (p. 85). This passage indicates a sophisticated understanding of the ways oppressed working-class groups are pitted against each other through manipulation of their economic situations.

Jefferson Cowie (2010) describes his experience teaching in a New York correctional facility and the depth of the students' class-based analysis:

> The questions came from every direction. How could Tom Joad, asked one, be the quintessential American working-class hero (as I had suggested) if Steinbeck had ignored the Asian and Mexican workers who had done most of the agricultural labor in California? Another, responding to how land got used in Oklahoma and California, asked if the constitutional system functioned in a way that enforced inequality.... An inmate even asked whether the dollar was grounded in human labor, and whether human labor can be considered a commodity like any other. (p.B20)

In many ways prisons are a microcosm of the larger society and one way is that they tend to be deeply segregated. It would be a liberal fairy tale to believe that race and class unity can be achieved through college courses. But education can serve as one factor of many toward creating a class consciousness that perceives the need for different groups to work together over common concerns. Says one prisoner, "As one Black dude said to me, Hey, look it, we've got to have respect for each other, but that doesn't mean you have to kiss me and I have to kiss you" (Linebaugh, 1995, p. 74).

<u>Women's Studies</u>
Comprising about 7% of those incarcerated in the United States, women represent a relatively small part of the overall prison population, comprising 161,000 inmates. Yet, the number of women prisoners is growing at a higher rate than for men. Between 2000 and 2007, the male inmate population grew 2.0% while the female population grew 3.2% (Sabol & Cuture, 2008). Like the men, women in prison tend to be low-income, under-educated, and people of color. In addition, they are often battered and otherwise abused. While all prisoners report a higher rate of abuse as youth than the general population, women prisoners report three times more than men. Prisons tend to be androcentric, making life challenging for female inmates. They face constant lack of privacy from the gaze of male guards even when performing very basic bodily functions (Irwin, 2005). Many of these women, having faced a lifetime of male domination find little respite in a correctional setting where they often face sexual abuse by the staff (Aday & Krabill, 2011; Ferro, 2011, Hudnall, 2011). Higher education can help these women to empower themselves to face the challenges of prison life. Prison educator Kristin Valentine (1998) suggests that it "gives incarcerated women a measure of mental control over their otherwise regimented bodies" (p.2). However, women in prison often meet the same kinds of barriers to education that they face on the outside, including discrimination based on gender. A nationwide study of educational offerings to female prisoners indicates that they are often limited to training in what are usually considered "women's work," such as secretarial, seamstress or service occupations (Lahm, 2010).

Some educators have recognized the needs of female inmates. A theater education program for women at the San Francisco County Jail utilizes Frierian methods to "explore their own marginalized [plight] and exploitation in a racist and classist society" (Olguin, 2010, P. 244). The theater company stages its program both with the inmates and for their families in order to help facilitate a dialogue regarding issues pertaining to interpersonal and macroscopic domination.

The first university level course taught in a woman's prison was in Women's Studies. In 1972 Karlene Faith and Jeanne Gallick organized a program at California's Institution for Women, then holding the distinction of having the largest population of female inmates in the world. "Women in Society" was the name of the course and it consisted of examination of women's roles in the family, education, the legal system, and the intersections and divisions related to race and class. Enrollment averaged about 100 students. They could receive credit in the University of California System. According to Faith (1995):

> [The program's mission] broke with all assumptions of traditional penal philosophy. We did not assume that the women were in need of rehabilitation. We understood crime as a socially constructed condition, and criminal justice as a discriminatory system that criminalized people from the least socially empowered groups. We rejected patriarchal and class based assumptions which stereotype women in conflict with the law as nonconformists to feminine standards. As program planners we did not presume to know better than the women inside what they needed to make sense of their lives. (p. 181)

The program at Santa Cruz eventually came to an end, in part due to burnout from the all-volunteer teaching staff who found the work load adversely affecting their finances and personal lives. Many innovative programs suffer the same fate when they rely on volunteer staff. Prisoners have few options to fill in the funding gap themselves. In a Michigan Women Studies prison program, the instructors state that inmates paying the tuition themselves "would be prohibitively expensive for women (whose 'jobs may pay as little as 27 cents per hour and from which they must purchase their own toiletries, like soap, shampoo, and deodorant) without further assistance" (Lembert, Bergeron & Linker, 2005, p. 200). Volunteer burnout and limited inmate resources combine to limit the availability of women's studies programs for those who may be in the most need of liberation: prisoners. Restoration of Pell Grant funding could help fill the gap where it is so badly needed. According to Lembert, Bergeron and Linker (2005), "We are continuously reminded about the limits and constraints on poor, uneducated, unskilled women and the particular burdens of women of color. But we are also discovering the varied ways that women in prison, who have the opportunity to participate in woman's studies coursework, form bonds of solidarity with other women" (p. 206).

<u>Ethnic Studies</u>
Ethnic Studies has had a long history in prisons, primarily of an informal nature. This is not surprising considering the criminal justice system in the U.S. is a racially charged construct. The high numbers of Black, Latino and Native Americans in prison relative to Whites is all too obvious to those even remotely familiar with the corrections system. The 1960s and 1970s Black and Chicano Power movements ushered in a flowering of formal and informal ethnic studies within prisons. Juan Rivera (1995) describes a program he and other prisoners set up at three New York State prisons to focus on Black and Latin Studies using what they termed the Nontraditional approach to correctional education. The courses consisted of three areas: Afrocentric, Latinocentric and Liberation Theology. The course content included an examination of cultural history, the socioeconomic conditions that give rise to the "crime-generative attitudes" of the inmates, as well as the role of social control and the local politics. From these foci the prisoners gain "insight into how he or she fits into the community, which instills a sense of responsibility toward the community and the people in it" (p.165). Rivera states that the prison administration had a certain level of opposition to the program based upon the goal of maintaining total control of the institution:

> The prison administrator's primary reason for opposing prisoners' programs is the need to maintain an image of control within the prison walls and to appear competent in the

public's eye. Prisoners must be viewed as dependent on state programs, which are created by the experts employed by the criminal justice system. Anything short of a state-run program is viewed with skepticism. This is especially true if the program is radically different... Some correctional officials believe in punishment rather than rehabilitation, and they view prison programs especially those created by prisoners, as ways to manipulate the system. (p.168)

A program exists at New York State's Sing Sing prison, which provides a Master's degree with an emphasis on community service. Academic work is combined with activities such as tutoring and volunteering in the prison hospital's AIDs ward. Manning Marable (1999), who taught in the program gave his impression: "I thought that the Black men I had met in Sing Sing prison were among the 'freest' people I knew. I feel more strongly about this than ever before. Freedom is a struggle that begins in one's mind. These African American men behind bars challenge themselves daily to live as free human beings. Their courage should inspire us to do the same" (p.80). Only about 5 percent of the program's participants returned to prison after being released compared to a statewide recidivism rate of 42 percent. The program's success cannot be measured purely through numbers, but also through its ability to emancipate the students' spirits. Unfortunately, graduate programs like the one at Sing Sing are quite rare and only 1.6 percent of Black state inmates have any kind of college degree (Harlow, 2003).

<u>Vocational Education</u>
Higher education does not necessarily pursue emancipatory goals. Colleges and universities have faced increasing pressure to offer vocational curricula in recent years. Even liberal arts programs have succumbed to global trends. According to Stoddard and Cornwell (2001), "in the context of globalized neoliberalism, liberal education has had to adopt market discourse to describe its work and justify its results" (p. 13). Giroux (2003) suggests that commodification of academic life has led to a culture whose message conflicts with the ideal goals of higher learning and supports an atmosphere where higher education serves primarily as entre' to the marketplace. Yet, despite its

current failings, Giroux holds on to the belief that higher education has the potential to serve "as an institution of civic culture whose purpose is to educate students for active and critical citizenship" (p. 188).

Is vocational education devoid of these possibilities? Can job training also advance intellectual and moral thinking in regards to issues of justice both in the workplace, and also for community at large? Can a critical pedagogy exist that sees the student not as a tool of the market; but as a whole person who, through reflection and experience, can change not only herself, but also her workplace, community and the nation? Simon, Dippo and Shenker (1991) have advocated for a pedagogy that seeks fairness in the work environment. Lakes (1994) calls for classrooms that "offer opportunities for the analysis of workplace issues as part of a broader cultural project involving learners in the resolution of inequality and injustice in our social institutions" (p.6).

In a previous chapter I discussed the New York state prison plumbing training program. How might critical pedagogy have helped reach those young men who dropped out of the program? Roger Simon (1991) suggests that a key step in the process of emancipatory education is a recognition of the "systemic social realities that influence how people view their work" (p. 14) and how these views are influenced by class, gender and age. Perhaps a good starting point might be to examine attitudes toward plumbers. What has been the historic contributions of the plumbing profession to the health and safety of society? How are plumbers currently portrayed in the media? Are they realistic or caricatures? What do these portrayals say about the attitudes of elites toward the working class or other groups who are not in power? This line of inquiry may help develop a more enlightened consciousness toward plumbers and other trades people, and perhaps encourage the young people toward realizing their attitudes toward working-class jobs may not have been based upon most plumbers' reality.

Adam Reich (2010) a prison educator who has worked with youths states that a critical pedagogy can help young prisoners reframe their basic outlook on life, "they reimagine power as the capacity to address their problems collectively through political praxis. And respect, formally 'won' through competition with other young men, becomes something akin to mutual recognition, or love" (P. 35).

In addition to vocational education, the stress on basic adult education in prisons is not without its advantages. After all, 41% of all U.S. prisoners do not possess a high school diploma or GED compared to 18% in the general population. One out of seven prisoners had not gone beyond the 8th grade (Harlow, 2003). Like vocational education, literacy programs in correctional facilities can be relevant and transformative. In his work, *Literacy with an Attitude* (1999), Patrick Finn suggests that teaching literacy from a transformative framework begins with the understanding that "proper communication between adults in a democracy is dialogue between equals" (p. 167). This starting point may be a challenge to both the teacher and the students, particularly in classrooms where there is often a wide gulf between the teacher and student, in terms of class position and educational attainment. One way to help facilitate democratic dialogue is through the cultivation of what Gramsci calls "organic intellectuals" whereby teachers arise from within the same or similar class as the students (Simon, 1991).

Paulo Freire, whom many consider the founder of critical pedagogy, grounded his ideas not in the hallowed halls of a prestigious university, nor through liberal arts curricula, but by teaching basic literacy to the poorest of the poor in the slums of Brazil, in the same kinds of situations that he spent his youth (Freire, 1970). The key to teaching literacy, according to Friere, is understanding the situation where the pedagogy occurs culturally and politically. Pedagogy must exist as a dialogue between student and teacher, otherwise the teacher is just "preaching in the desert" (p. 96). One prisoner education model that exemplifies the Frierian approach is the Inside-Out program based out of Temple University. The program utilizes a method based upon dialogue between students who happen to be in prison and teachers and students at the university. Thus, it seeks to avoid the "banking" style of pedagogy in which the teacher deposits information into the student. Classes with both inmate and non-inmate students meet in the prison. The university students obtain insight into lived experiences of the inmates and are able to move past stereotypes. The imprisoned students gain academic confidence through participation in the program. According to coordinator Lori Pompa (2011): "The process challenges everyone involved to work through their assumptions about others and their imposed limitations on themselves... to begin the long road toward social justice" (p.257). Since its origin in 1997, over 7,500 inmates and non-inmates have participated in the program.

While it is no extraordinary leap to imagine how Friere's ideas could translate to America's penal institutions, according to Michael Collins, (1995) "The main difficulties await the Freirean approach in the prison as prevail on the outside" (p. 60). These include opposition from the administration, subversion of Friere's call for social transformation and a tendency to value functionalism. These obstacles can be overcome. A critical pedagogy can lead students to seek fundamental change to an unjust social structure. Alexandria Mageehon (2008) uses Frierian techniques in prison education so that she can "lead others to question the status quo of our society - to think, to question, and to act to change the system" (p. 48). A system that results in the world's highest prison rate cries out for change.

The primary goal of this section is not to establish a template or a specific set of curricular goals for prison education, but rather to shed light on the possibilities that may arise if prisoners and teachers have some control over education. The prison education programs described above are remarkable in their boldness as well as their diversity in content and methodology, but one commonality is that they tend to be limited in either their enrollment or their lifespan due to funding cuts or limitations. Typical is the correctional education project involving the University of Pittsburgh. Initiated by a request from state prisoners, the program began in the 1970s. The project involved faculty from the Black Studies, the Communication and the Psychology Departments. Educators Monica Frolander-Ulf and Michael Yates (2001) describe its funding challenges:

> The tuition costs were initially financed through Pell Grants. When Congress decided to deny these grants to prisoners in 1994, Pitt began charging each student a per-credit fee, and those serving life sentences were charged the full cost of in-state tuition. In 1994, [the year inmate Pell Grants were cut off] the word came from Harrisburg that the program was to be terminated within a few years. No new students were to be enrolled and the program was to target those students who would be able to graduate before its termination. The administration issued a new set of requirements for prisoner

education, which was to include basic education, certificate, business and career development programs only. In 1998, the Pitt College Program was shut down. (p. 120)

The above passage brings up a very good point regarding the link between the end of Pell Grants for prisoners and the increase in basic education.   The situation at Pitt was not an isolated occurrence. According to the U.S. Department of Justice, in state prisons, where a majority of prisoners are housed, the number that offered college courses declined from 31.4 percent to 26.7 percent from 1995 to 2000. This reduction apparently was not without an effect, for state inmates having some college decreased from 10.1% to 9.0 % in the same decade (Harlow, 2003). While adult basic education is important, for the one half of prisoners who already hold a GED or high school degree, it may not help create the informed, active citizens found in the previously described programs for prisoners if taught purely from a functionalist perspective. According to Joan Steiner (2001), "To maintain a democracy, education for all people is essential if they are to participate in sociopolitical decision making" (p. 153). It is not just any kind of education. Steiner and others (Friere, 2004; Giroux, 2006, Carr, 2011) advocate for participatory and emancipatory pedagogy that seeks to bridge the gap between those who are within the loop and those who are not. A functionalist education within an individualized, neoliberal framework is unlikely to reach this goal. As Simone Davis (2011) suggests, prisoner pedagogy can only be emancipatory if education undergoes a "radical reconceptualization: a redefinition that emphasizes community creation and collective purpose rather than individual self-'betterment' and 'upward' mobility" (p.206).

Involvement in social action can have a positive effect upon the inmates. A study by Thomas LeBel (2009) indicates that former inmates who become engaged in social justice issues are less likely to commit crimes after release. The research involved 229 male and female prisoners and examined the correlation between a social activist orientation and positive re-entry. Those inmates who were either collectively working or willing to work to improve the conditions of themselves and their fellow inmates were much less likely to believe that breaking the law was a good way to get ahead in the world than those inmates who were not social activists. Based on the findings,

LeBel suggests that there is a "basic incompatibility between an advocacy/activism orientation and criminal attitudes and behavior" (p. 182).

Critical pedagogy can help the students take a more active role in reshaping both their own lives and the world around them. Emancipatory education that serves marginalized communities can be enhanced by funding sources with few curricular restrictions attached, such as the Pell Grant. While a few truly transformative programs, such as the Inside-Out initiative have been able to survive or even prosper in the post-prisoner Pell Grant environment, their fate is less assured in the recent era of cuts in non-profit and university funding. Pell Grants provide a relatively steady source of educational funding that should be restored to prisoners.

Pell Grants are not inherently emancipatory. Taken in context of the overall thrust of education in the U.S., the Pell is just as likely to enhance and maintain societal hierarchies through the transmission of hegemonic values in the classroom as it is to facilitate positive social change. But compared to the content restrictions inherent in the Second Chance Act funding mechanism, which apparently require approval of course curriculum at the highest levels of the federal government, the lack of curricular strings attached to the Pell Grant at least makes possible small pockets of resistance to unjust dominant ideologies.

The issue of prisoner Pell Grants has remained the focus of several advocacy groups in the years since it was eliminated. In 2009, a coalition of civil liberties organizations, including the American Civil Liberties Union, American Bar Association and Human Rights Watch formed a legislative agenda for the new President and Congress that called for changes in the criminal justice system. Their demands included restoration of Pell Grants for prisoners (The 2009 Criminal Justice Coalition, 2009). Other groups have taken up the call for prisoner Pell Grants. They include the American Indian Higher Education Consortium, the NAACP, the Institute for Higher Education Policy, the Hispanic Association of Colleges and Universities, and the Correctional Education Association. The NAACP national convention approved a resolution encouraging "all units and members meet with and educate and urged Congress to restore prisoners Pell Grant eligibility" (Buford, 2008, P. 1). Congress should heed their call.

Critical pedagogy can be vital for the prisoners. They have experienced not the sweet fruits, but the poison berries of the nation in which they live. Thus, the incarcerated have a higher stake in assuming the reigns of change. Unfortunately, they are often denied the very means to enact those changes in a democratic manner. In the 2008 election, over 5.3 million former prisoners were denied the right to vote, to exercise their basic rights as citizens (Cohen, 2008). Yet, the greater disenfranchisement may come from the denial of the opportunities that education can offer to open minds to the world of possibility. Within the current policy framework, prisoners are viewed as capable of agency only within a narrow market-oriented lens of basic adult education and job training.

In his 1994 State of the Union, President Bill Clinton stated:

> [Our nation can] put our economic house in order, expand world trade, target the jobs of the future, guarantee equal opportunity, but if we're honest, we'll all admit that this strategy still cannot work unless we also give our people the education, training, and skills they need to seize the opportunities of tomorrow. (as cited in C-SPAN.org, 1994)

The same year in which he made this speech, Clinton signed into law the legislation denying Pell Grants for prisoners. Apparently they were not considered "our people."

Future Research

There are several avenues to extend this study. The scope of this work was confined primarily to the adult prison population and education initiatives focused on this group. Juvenile inmates tend to be afforded more educational opportunities than adults. Follow-up studies could apply many of the same questions to youth inmates, including the prevalence and appropriateness of critical pedagogy. Like the Second Chance Act for adults, comprehensive legislation has also been proposed for incarcerated youth. They include the Youth Prison Reduction through Mentoring, Intervention, Support and Education Act, otherwise known as the Youth Promise Act (Scott, 2009). An analysis of the implications of this legislation would be helpful.

There should be more follow up on how the Second Chance Act is implemented, including the processes of job training and mentoring. Particular interest should be paid to which organizations actually receive grants, what programs they propose, how they are carried out and their effects on the participants. During congressional hearings surrounding the 2010 reauthorization of the Second Chance Act, Bobby Scott (D-VA) rightly concluded that the timespan since initial passage was insufficient to judge effectiveness: "One of the problems we have with the Second Chance Act programs is that funding of the programs has not been made available long enough for the programs to show enough activity and results to credibly evaluate their impact" (Scott, 2011 p. 1). Prisoner re-entry is a big issue and the solution is likely to be measured in decades rather than years.

Follow-up research should include longitudinal studies utilizing both quantitative and qualitative techniques. Viewpoints of current and former prisoners and classroom teachers should be considered in this evaluation. In addition, the input of other stakeholders including the families of prisoners should be valued. The Second Chance Act contains provisions that establish studies to examine the impact of the legislation on prisoner re-entry. The sole criterion for successful prisoner re-entry is recidivism rates. The number of former inmates who reenter the prison system is an important area of study. However, there are other aspects of the post-release experience that should also be examined. These include employment rates, level of income, as well as the ability to obtain adequate housing. Additionally, there are criteria that could relate to successful re-entry that extend beyond the economic realm. How do the men and women perceive themselves? Are they happy or not? Have they become integrated into the social lives of their families or their communities? Do they take leadership roles in these environments? Have they successfully made the transition from maintenance to becoming agents of change in themselves, their families or their communities? Have they come to recognize the "crime generative" aspects of their communities and the larger society, and begun working to effect positive change? These are all questions that can and should be a part of the overall research approach to prisoner re-entry. The answers to these questions would be helpful in understanding the efficacy of re-entry programs in helping prisoners reincorporate into their communities in a beneficial, sustainable manner.

Conclusion

With the highest incarceration rate of any nation, the United States and its justice system have reached a state of crisis. The massive costs associated with warehousing 2 million prisoners, has begun to burden already financially strapped federal and state governments. This places pressure on the policymakers to find lower-cost alternatives that would still maintain carceral control over these men, women and children. At a glance, the Second Chance Act seems to contradict limited government aspects of the dominant neoliberal philosophy given the characterization as a massive government program designed to help those in prison. The dichotomy ends when the legislation is carefully unpacked; it appears to serve as a means to privatize government services through public private partnerships. Perhaps as important, if not more so than the financial costs was the crisis of legitimacy. All oppressive systems thrive on an aura of legitimacy. Several factors threaten the reputation of the American criminal justice system including its high incarceration rates, high recidivism rates and its disproportional effect on the poor and people of color. In order to countermand these realities, a narrative that seemingly combines the traits of compassion, toughness and efficiency was created. This was a tricky proposition. But by allowing politicians representing a wide spectrum of political perspectives to have a voice in the debate, each trait was represented in the discourse, at least rhetorically; if not in the reality of the legislation's provisions. Policy representing such a wide range of interests invariably is suffused with contradictions. A contradiction exists between the reality of the disciplinary aspects of the Second Chance re-entry programs and the neoliberal myth of personal freedom. These programs can function to control former prisoner's lives even as they are considered "free." Rather than helping to facilitate truly free and just lives, the Act appears to perpetuate hierarchy enhancing constructs of the society that marginalize groups of people. Some of the aspects of the Second Chance Act, such as healthcare and transitional housing represent a movement of welfare into the domain of criminal justice and are certainly needed. However, unless their funding is greatly increased, they are likely to serve merely as window dressing by providing legitimacy to the more disciplinary aspects of the policy. Legitimacy is enhanced through debate rhetoric which defines success solely within the confines of the marketplace. By largely excluding alternative ways of seeing the world, such as those embedded in the need for social justice and community, the debate appears to promote a very narrow view of re-entry.

The women and men who are in prison will never have the chance to be truly free, if even after they are released, they are forced to live the rest of their lives under the gaze of a legal system that regulates just about every part of their existence. They are restricted in how they work via vocational tracking and their criminal records, and their values may be force fed through mandatory mentoring. The Second Chance Act appears to function as a disciplinary regime that denies the potential of these men and women to create their own place in society as engaged, caring, free agents.

Funding for re-entry programs will not solve all the problems of the women and men who have been impacted by our nation's penal system. Much of the challenge they face, as described in this study, is due to an economic system that is generally unforgiving to those on the edge of society. An alternative vision of the future can be realized through emancipatory education which recognizes and values the special role that learners play in defining their place in the world. Let's give these women and men that chance.

References

ABC News.com. (2008, February 24). Dem govs look for ways to manage 'explosion' of prisoners leaving jail. *ABC News*. Retrieved (October 2, 2008) from http://blogs.abcnews.com/politicalradar/2008/02/dem-govs-look-f.html.

Aday, R. & Krabill, J. (2011). *Women aging in prison: A neglected population in the correctional system.* Boulder, CO: Lynne Reinner Publishers.

Alexander, M. (2010). *The new Jim Crow: Mass incarceration in the age of colorblindness.* New York: New Press.

Alexander, M. (2011). Throwing away the key. *The Sun,* Issue 422.

Allard, P. & Greene, J. (2011). Children on the outside: Voicing the pain and human costs of parental incarceration. Brooklyn, N.Y.: *Justice Strategies.* Retrieved March 22, 2011 from http://www.justicestrategies.org/sites/default/files/publications/JS-COIP-1-13-11.pdf.

Anderson, E. (2001). Going straight: The story of a young inner-city ex-convict. In D. Garland (Ed.), *Mass Imprisonment: Social causes and consequences* (pp. 121-137). London: Sage Publications.

Antonio, E. (2007). Black theology. In C. Rowland (Ed.), *The Cambridge companion to liberation theology* (2nd ed.). (pp.79 – 104). Cambridge: Cambridge University Press.

Associated Press. (2009, January 10). States ponder early release for prisoners. *MSNBC.com.* Retrieved January 11, 2009, from http://www.msnbc.msn. com/id28592088/print/1/displaymode/10981.

Barrett, K. (March 13, 2008). CBC: The congressional black caucus lauds senate on the passage of the second chance act of 2007. *Targeted News Service.* Retrieved September 9, 2008 from http://wf2dnvr14.webfeat.org.

Bauman, Z. (2001). *The individualized society*. Cambridge UK: Polity Press.

Bauer, J. & Chivakos, A. (2010). What's Islam got to do with it? American pluralism, ethnographic sensibilities, and faith-based refugee resettlement in Hartford, Connecticut. In J. Adkins, L. Occhipinti, T. Hefferan (Eds.), *Not by faith alone: Social services, social justice, and faith-based organizations in the United States* (pp. 145 – 164). Lanham, MD: Lexington Books.

Bernstein, L. (2010). *America is the prison: Arts and politics in prison in the 1970s.* Chapel Hill: University of North Carolina Press.

Biden, J. Sen. (1993). Violent crime control and law enforcement act of 1993. *Congressional Record* (Senate - November 17, 1993) Page: S15967.

Biden, J. Sen. (2004). Statements on introduced bills and joint resolutions. *Congressional Record* (Senate - October 07, 2004) Page: S10717.

Biden, J. Sen. (2004). Statements on introduced bills and joint resolutions --*Congressional Record* (Senate October 07, 2004) Page: S10718.

Black, A. E., Koopman, D. L., & Ryden, D. K. (2004). *Of little faith: The politics of George W. Bush's faith-based initiatives.* Washington, DC: Georgetown University Press.

Blackburn, M. Rep. (2007). Oppose the second chance act. *Congressional Record* (House of Representatives - May 16, 2007) Page: H5286.

Blomberg, T. G. & Lucken, K. (2010). *American penology: A history of control.* New Brunswick, NJ: Transaction Publishers.

Bloom, B. (1995). Imprisoned mothers. In K. Gabel & D. Johnston (Eds.), *Children of incarcerated parents* (pp. 21 – 30). New York: Lexington Books.

Bogdan, R. & Biklen, S. (2003). *Qualitative research for education: An introduction to theories and methods.* Boston: Allyn and Bacon.

Boren, S. (1989). The pell grant program: Background and issues. *Congressional Research Service Report.* Washington, DC: Library of Congress, Congressional Research Service.

Boswell, G. & Wedge, P. (2002). *Imprisoned fathers and their children.* London: Jessica Kingsley Publishers.

Bosworth, M. (2010). *Explaining U. S. imprisonment.* Thousand Oaks, CA: Sage Publications.

Boudin, K. & Zeller-Berkman, S. (2010). Children of promise. In Y. Harris, J. Graham, G. Carpenter (Eds.), *Children of incarcerated* parents: Theoretical, developmental, and clinical issues* (pp. 73–101). New York: Springer Publishing.

Briscoe, F. (2000). Discipline. In D. Gabbard (Ed.), *Knowledge and power in the global economy: Politics and the rhetoric of school reform* (pp. 63 - 68). Mahwah, NJ: Lawrence Erlbaum Associates.

Brownback, S. Sen. (2008). Second chance act. *Congressional Record.* Senate - April 10, 2008) Page: S2938.

Burford, J. (June, 2008). Restoration of prisoner's pell grant eligibility overdue. *The Prison Mirror.* Retrieved March 3, 2009 from http://www.realcostofprisons.org /materials/pellgrant.pdf.

Burger, W. E. (1985). On education in prison. In S. Chaneles, (Ed.), *Prisons and prisoners: Historical documents* (pp 193-194). New York: The Haworth Press, Inc.

Burns, R. (2000). *Introduction to research methods.* London: Sage Publications.

Bush, G. W. (2008). Remarks on signing the second chance act of 2007. *Weekly Compilation of Presidential Documents.* 44(14) 503–505. Retrieved January 9, 2009 from http://wf2dnvr14.webfeat.org/wmcLL768/url=http://proguestumi.com.

Cannon, C. Rep. (2007). Second chance act of 2007. *Congressional Record.* (House of Representatives - November 13, 2007) Page: H13582.

Carr, P. (2011) *Does your vote count? Critical pedagogy and democracy.* New York: Peter Lang.

Carter, J. Rep. (2007). Oppose the second chance act. *Congressional Record* (House of Representatives - May 16, 2007) Page: H5284.

Carter, J. & Gohmert, L. Rep. (2007). Oppose the second chance act. *Congressional Record* (House of Representatives - May 16, 2007) Page: H5284.

Chambers, C.L. (2011). *Drug laws and institutional racism: The story Told by the congressional record.* El Paso, TX: LFB Scholarly Publishing LLC.

Chambliss, W. J. (1999). *Power, politics and crime.* Boulder, CO: Westview Press.

Chiricos, T. (1996). Moral panics as ideology: Drugs, violence, race and punishment in America. In C. Critcher (Ed.), *Critical readings: Moral panics and the media* (pp. 103 – 123). Berkshire, UK: Open University Press.

Chiricos, T., Eschholz, S., & Gertz, M. (2006). Crime, news and fear of crime: Toward an identification of audience effects In G.W. Potter and K.E. Kappeler (Eds.), *Constructing crime: Perspectives on making news and social problems.* (pp. 269–287). Long Grove, IL: Waveland Press, Inc.

Christian, S. (2009). Children of incarcerated parents. *National Conference of state legislatures.* Retrieved January 12, 2011 from http://www.ncsl.org/documents/cyf/childrenofincarceratedparents. pdf.

Chung, H. and McFadden, D. (2010). The effects of incarceration on neighborhoods and communities. In Y. Harris, J. Graham, G. Carpenter (Eds.), *Children of incarcerated parents: Theoretical, developmental, and clinical issues* (pp. 105-126). New York: Springer Publishing.

Chura, D. (2010). *I don't wish nobody to have a life like mine: Tales of kids in adult lockup.* Boston: Beacon Press.

Cohen, A. (2008). Ex-felon voters foiled by confused officials. *National Public Radio.* Retrieved October 8, 2008 from http://www.npr.org/ templates/story/story.php? Story ID = 95509755.

Cole, M. (2005). New labour, globalization, and social justice: The role of education. In G. Fischman, P. McLaren, H. Sunker and C. Lankshear (Eds.), *Critical theories, Radical pedagogies and global conflicts* (pp. 3-22). Lanham MA: Rowan and Littlefield.

Coley, R. and Barton, P. (2006). Locked Up and Locked Out: An Educational Perspective on the U.S. Prison Population. *Educational Testing Service.* Retrieved October 15, 2010 from http://www.ets. org/Media/Research/pdf/PIC-LOCKEDUP.pdf.

Collins, M. (1995). Shades of the prison house: Adult literacy and the correctional ethos. In H. Davidson (Ed.), *Schooling in a total institution: Critical perspectives on prison education* (pp. 49 – 64). Westport, CT: Bergin and Garvey.

Congressional Black Caucus (May, 2011). Our mission. *Congressional Black Caucus Newsletter,* p. 2.

Congressional Quarterly. Duncan, P. (Ed.). (1993). *CQ's Politics in America 1994: 103rd Congress Washington, DC: CQ Press.*

Congressional Quarterly. Koszczuk, J., & Stern, H. (Eds.). (2005). *CQ's Politics in America 2006: The 109th Congress.* Washington, DC: CQ Press.

Congressional Quarterly. (2008). *How Congress Works* (4th ed.). Washington, DC: CQ Press.

Conley, D. & Debro, J. (2002). Black muslims in california prisons: The beginning of a social movement for black prisoners in the United States. In C. Reasons, D.Conley and J. Debro (Eds.), *Race, class, gender and justice in the United States* (pp. 278-291). Boston, MA: Allyn and Bacon.

Conyers, J. Rep. (1992). Higher education amendments of 1992. *Congressional Record* (House of Representatives - March 26, 1992 H1895.

Conyers, J. Rep. (2003). Introduction of civic participation and rehabilitation act of 2003 Hon John Conyers, Jr. *Congressional Record* (Extensions of Remarks - January 08, 2003) Page: E40.

Cook, B. J. and King, J. E. (2007). *2007 status report on the pell grant program.* Washington, DC: American Council on Education.

Coven, M. (2005). *An introduction to TANF.* Washington, DC: Center on Budget and Policy Priorities.

Covington, S. (2003). A woman's journey home: Challenges for female offenders. In J. Travis and M. Waul (Eds.), *Prisoners once removed: The impact of incarceration and reentry on children, families, and communities* (pp.67 – 104). Washington, DC: Urban Institute Press.

Cowie, J., (2010). Lecturing in a prison, where minds are free. *Chronicle of Higher Education,* 56 (24) B20.

Critcher, C. (2006). Introduction: More questions than answers. In C. Critcher (Ed.), *Critical readings: Moral panics and the media* (pp. 1 – 14). Berkshire, UK: Open University Press.

Cummings, E. Rep. (2007). Second Chance Act. *Congressional Record* (House of Representatives - November 13, 2007) Page: H13829.

C-SPAN.org (1994). President Bill Clinton's address on the state of the union. *C-SPAN.* Retrieved October 26, 2008 from http://www.cspan. org/executive /transcript.asp?cat=current_event&code=bush_admin &year=1994.

Davis, D. Rep. (2007). Everyone deserves a second chance. *Congressional Record* (House of Representatives - May 23, 2007) Page: H5691.

Davis, S. (2011). Inside-out: The reaches and limits of a prison program. In J. Lawston and A. Lucas (Eds.), *Razor wire women: Prisoners, activists, scholars and artists.* (pp. 203-223). New York: State University of New York Press.

Davidson, H. S. (1995). Possibilities for critical pedagogy in a "total institution": An introduction to critical perspectives on prison education. In H. S. Davidson (Ed.), *Schooling in a "total institution": Critical perspectives on prison education.* (pp. 1 – 24). Westport, CT: Bergin and Garvey.

Difazio, W. (2003). Time, poverty and global democracy. In S.Aronowitz and H. Gautney (Eds.), *Implicating empire: Globalization and resistance in the 21st century world order* (pp. 159 - 178). New York: Basic Books.

Dornan, R. Rep. (1994). Improving America's schools act of 1994. *Congressional Record* (House of Representatives - March 24, 1994) Page: H2026.

Dornan, R. Rep. (1994). The validity of the whitewater investigation. *Congressional Record* (House of Representatives - April 21, 1994) Page: H2627.

Dornan, R. Rep. (1994). The validity of the whitewater investigation. *Congressional Record* (House of Representatives - April 21, 1994) Page: H2628.

Dror, Y. (1962). Policy analysts: A new professional role in government service. In J. Shafritz, A. Hyde and S. Parkes (Eds.), *Classics of public administration* (pp. 250 – 257). Boston: Thomson Wadsworth.

Du Buff, R. (2002). A slippery slope: Economists and social insurance in the United States. In V. Navarro (Ed.), *The political economy of social inequities: Consequences for health and quality of life* (pp. 311-321). Amityville, NY: Baywood Publishing.

Dye, T. (1981). *Understanding public policy.* Englewood Cliffs, NJ: Prentice-Hall.

Eckholm, E. (2008, April 8). U.S. Shifting Prison Focus to Re-entry Into Society. *The New York Times.* Retrieved April 14, 2008, from http://www.nytimes.com/2008/04/08/washington/08reentry.html.

Eggleston, C. & Gehring, T. (2000). Democracy and prison education. *The Journal of Correctional Education.* 51 (3) 306 – 310.

Erisman, W. & Contardo, J. (2005). Learning to reduce recidivism: A 50- state analysis of postsecondary correctional policy. *The Institute of Higher Education Policy.* Retrievied February 12, 2009 From http://www.ihep.org/assets/files/publications/g-l/Learning ReduceRecidivism.pdf

Fairclough, A. (2001). *Better day coming: Blacks and equality: 1890-*

2000. New York: Penguin Books.

Fairclough, N. (1995). *Critical discourse analysis: The critical study of language*. London: Longman.

Faith, M. (1995). The Santa Cruz women's prison project, 1972 – 1976. In H. S. Davidson (Ed.), *Schooling in a "total Institution": Critical perspectives on prison education* (pp. 173 – 192). Westport, CT: Bergin and Garvey.

Favro T. (2007). Up to 10 million American children suffer the consequences of convicted parents. *City Mayors Society*. Retrieved September 23, 2008 from http://www.citymayorscom/society/usa-prisoners-children.html.

Ferro, J. (2011) *Prisons*. New York: Facts on File.

Fields, J. Rep. (1994). Amendment offered by Mr. Hunter. *Congressional Record* (House of Representatives - April 20, 1994) Page: H2545.

Finn, P. (1999). *Literacy with an attitude: Educating working-class children in their self-interest*. Albany: State University of New York Press.

Formicola, J. R., Segers, M. C., & Weber, P. (2003). *Faith-based initiatives and the Bush administration*. Lanham: Rowman & Littlefield Publishers, Inc.

Foucault, M. (1995). *Discipline and punish: The birth of the prison*. New York: Vintage Books.

Frenkel, S. (2006). Towards a theory of dominant interests, globalization and work. In M. Korczynski, R. Hodson and P. Edwards (Eds.), *Social theory at work* (pp. 388-423). Oxford: Oxford University Press.

Friedman, M. (1953). Choice, chance and the personal distribution of income. *The Journal of Political Economy*, 61(4) 277-290.

Friere, P. (1970). *Pedagogy of the oppressed*. New York: Continuum.

Friere, P. (2004). *Pedagogy of indignation*. Boulder, Co: Paradigm Publishers.

Frolander-Ulf, M. and Yates, M. (2001). Teaching in prison. *Monthly Review*, 53 (3) 114 – 128.

Gabbidon, S. (2010). *Race, ethnicity, crime and justice: An international dilemma*. Thousand Oaks, CA: Sage Publications.

Gallup, G. (1994). *The Gallup Poll, No. 341*, Wilmington, DL: Scholarly Resources.

Garland, D. (2001). Introduction: The meaning of mass imprisonment. *Punishment and society*, 3 (1) 5 – 7.

Gee, J. (2005). *Introduction to discourse analysis*. New York: Routledge.

Gehring, T., & Wright, R. (2003). Three ways of summarizing correctional educational progress trends. *Journal of Correctional Education*, 54 (1), 5-13.

Gehring, T. (2000). Recidivism as a measure of correctional education program success, *Journal Of Correctional Education*, (51) 2, 197-199.

Germanotta, D. (1995). Prison education: A contextual analysis. In H. S. Davidson (Ed.), *Schooling in a "total institution": Critical perspectives on prison education* (pp. 103 - 122). Westport, CT: Bergin and Garvey.

Gest, T. (2001). *Crime & Politics*. Oxford: Oxford University Press.

Gillespie, E. & Schellhas, B. (Eds.) (1994). *Contract with America*. New York: Times Books.

Giroux, H. (2003). *The abandoned generation: Democracy beyond the culture of fear*. New York: Palgrave MacMillan.

Giroux, H. (2006). *The Giroux reader*. Boulder, CO: Paradigm Publishers.

Glaze, L. E. (2010). Correctional populations in the United States, 2009. *Bureau of Justice Statistics Bulletin* NCJ 231681.

Glaze, L. E. & Maruschak, L. M. (2010). Parents in Prison and their minor children. *Bureau of Justice Statistics Special Report*. Revised 3/30/10 NCJ 222984.

Goffman, E. (1961). *Asylums: Essays on the social situation of mental patients and other inmates*. New York: Anchor.

Gohmert, L. Rep. (2007). Oppose the second chance act. *Congressional Record* (House of Representatives - May 16, 2007) Page: H5283.

Gohmert, L. Rep. (2007). Oppose the second chance act. *Congressional Record* (House of Representatives - May 16, 2007) Page: H5284.

Gohmert, L. Rep. (2007). Second chance act of 2007. *Congressional Record* (House of Representatives - November 13, 2007) Page: H13580.

Golden, R. (2005). *War on the family*. New York: Routledge.

Goode, E. & Ben-Yehuda, N. (1994). *Moral panics: The social construction of deviance*. Oxford, UK: Blackwell Publishing.

Goodling, B. Rep. (1992). Higher education amendments of 1992. *Congressional Record* (House of Representatives - March 26, 1992) Page: H1893.

Gordon, B. Rep. (1992). Higher education amendments of 1992. *Congressional Record* (House of Representatives - March 26, 1992) Page: H1893.

Gordon, C. (1991). Government rationality: An introduction. In G. Burchell, C. Gordon, & P. Miller (Eds.), *The Foucault effect* (pp. 1 – 52). Chicago: The University of Chicago Press.

Gordon, H. & Weldon, B. (2003). The impact of career and technical education programs on adult offenders learning behind bars. *The Journal of Correctional Education*, 54 (4) 200 – 209.

Gray, R. (November17, 2010). Seeds of Hope receives grant for jail ministry. *Garden City Telegram*. Retrieved March 2, 2011 from http://www. gctelegram.com/news/ jail-ministry- grant-11-17-10.

Graham, J., Harris Y., and Carpenter, G. (2010). The changing landscape in the American prison population: Implications for children of incarcerated parents. In Y. Harris, J. Graham, G. Carpenter (Eds.), *Children of incarcerated parents: Theoretical, developmental, and clinical issues* (pp. 3-20). New York: Springer Publishing.

Grbich, C. (2007). *Qualitative data analysis: An introduction.* Sage Publications: London.

Greene, J. (2002). Entrepreneurial corrections: Incarceration as a business opportunity. In M. Mauer and M. Chesney-Lind (Eds.) *Invisible punishment: The collateral consequences of mass imprisonment* (pp. 95-113). New York: The New Press.

Greenhouse, S. (January 24, 2011). States help ex-inmates find jobs. *New York Times*. Retrieved February 11, 2011 from http://www .nytimes.com/2011/01/25/business/25offender.html.

Gunderson, S. Rep. (1992). Higher education amendments of 1992. *Congressional Record* (House of Representatives - March 26, 1992) Page: H1896.

Hall, R. & Bannatyne, M. (2000). Technology education and the convicted felon: How it works behind prison walls. *The Journal of Correctional Education*, 51(4) 320 – 323.

Harlow, C. W. (2003). Education and correctional populations. *Bureau of Justice Statistics, Special Report*. NCJ 195670. Washington, DC: U.S. Department of Justice, Bureau of Justice Statistics.

Harlow, C. W., Jenkins, H. D., Steurer, S. (2010). GED holders in prison read better than those in the household population: Why? *The Journal of Correctional Education*, 61 (1)68.

Harold, C. (2007). *Our space: Resisting the corporate control of culture.* Minneapolis: University of Minnesota Press.

Harris, D. A. (1993). What happened to crime. *ABA Journal*, 79, 138.

Hart, R. & Moutos, T. (1995). *Human capital, employment and bargaining.* Cambridge: Cambridge University Press.

Harcourt, B. (2011). *The illusion of free markets: Punishment and the myth of natural order.* Cambridge, MA: Harvard University Press.

Hartog, J. & Oosterbeek, H. (2007). What do we know about the private returns to education. In J.Hartog and H. Massen van den Brink (Eds.) *Human capital: Advances in theory and evidence* (pp.7 - 20) Cambridge: Cambridge University Press.

Harvey, D. (2005). *A brief history of neoliberalism.* Oxford UK: Oxford University Press.

Henningsen, R., Johnson, W. and Wells, T. (2010). Supermax prisons: Panacea or desperation? In E. Latessa and A. Holsinger (Eds.) *Correctional contexts: Contemporary and classical readings* (pp.78-85). New York: Oxford University Press.

Hohenberg, J. (1997). *Reelecting Bill Clinton: Why America Chose a "New" Democrat.* Syracuse: Syracuse University Press.

Honan, W. H. (2009). Claiborne Pell, ex-senator, dies at 90. *The New York Times.* Retrieved January 2, 2009 from http://www.nytimes.com/009/ 01/ 02/us/politics/02pell.html

Hrabowski, F. A. & Robbi, J. (2002). The benefits of correctional education. *Journal of Correctional Education,* 53 (3) 96 – 100.

Hudnall, J. (2011). Prison rape. In J. Lawston and A. Lucas (Eds.), *Razor wire women: Prisoners, activists, scholars and artists* (pp. 165-168). New York: State University of New York Press.

Hutchison, K. B. Sen. (1993). Violent crime control and law enforcement act. *Congressional Record* (Senate - November 10, 1993) Page: S15586.

Hutchison, K.B. Sen. (1993). Violent crime control and law enforcement act of 1993. *Congressional Record* (Senate –November 16, 1993) Page: S15748.

Hutchison, K. B. Sen. (1993). Violent crime control and law enforcement act of 1993. *Congressional Record.* (Senate –November 16, 1993) Page: S15746.

Irwin, J. (2005). *The warehouse prison: Disposal of the new dangerous class.* Los Angeles: Roxbury Publishing.

Jackson-Lee, S. Rep. (2007). The second chance act of 2007.*Congressional Record* (Extensions of Remarks - December 18, 2007) Page: E2597.

James, T. (1988). Totality in private and public schooling. *American Journal of Education,* 97 (1) 1 – 17.

Jayasuriya, K. (2006). *Statecraft, welfare and the politics of inclusion.* New York: Palgrave MacMillan

Johnston, D. (1995) Effects of parental incarceration. In K. Gabel and D. Johnston (Eds.), *Children of incarcerated parents* (pp. 59-88). New York: Lexington Books.

Justice Policy Institute (2002). *Cellblocks or classrooms?: The funding of higher education and corrections and its impact on African American men.* Washington, DC: Justice Policy Institute.

Kaiser, M. (2010). Correctional Education, because it works. *Corrections Today,* 72 (4) 18 -20.

Kalunta-Crumpton, A. (2010). In Conclusion: Comparative assessment of race, crime and criminal justice in international perspectives. In *A.* Kalunta-Crumpton (Ed*.), Race, crime and criminal justice: International perspectives.* (pp. 309 – 325). New York: Palgrave Macmillan.

Kelly, P. (2006). The entrepreneurial self and 'youth at-risk': Exploring the horizons of identity in the twenty-first century. *Journal of Youth Studies,* 9 (1) 17 – 32.

Kennedy, E. (2007). Recidivism reduction and second chance act of 2007- *Congressional Record* (Senate - April 12, 2007) Page: S4431.

Kincheloe, J. (2008). *Critical pedagogy primer.* New York: Peter Lang.

King, J. (2000). Race. In D. Gabbard (Ed.) *Knowledge and power in the global economy: Politics and the rhetoric of school reform* (pp. 141-148). Mahwah N.J: Lawrence Erlbaum Associates.

King James Version. (n.d.). *The holy bible.* Cleveland, OH: World Publishing Company.

Kolko, G. (2002). Ravaging the poor: The international monetary fund indicted by its own data. In V. Navarro (Ed.) *The political economy of social inequities: Consequences for health and quality of life* (pp. 173 - 180). Amityville, NY: Baywood Publishing.

Kondracke, M. (September 19, 1994). Crime bill wasn't just pork as tv documentary shows. *Roll Call.* Retrieved February 2, 2009 from http://ezproxy.gsu.edu:2650/us/lnacademic/results/docview/doc view.do?docLinkInd=true&risb=21_T5875906040&format=GNBF I&sort=BOOLEAN&startDocNo=1&resultsUrlKey=29_T5875906 043&cisb=22_T5875906042&treeMax=true&treeWidth=&csi=3 624&docNo=20.

Kotz, D. (2011) Financialization and neoliberalism. In G. Teeple and S.

McBride (Eds.), *Relations of global power: Neoliberal order and disorder* (pp. 1-18) Toronto:University of Toronto Press.

Kravitz, W. (1993). *Congressional Quarterly's American Congressional Dictionary*. Washington, DC: Congressional Quarterly, Inc.

Krisberg, B. (2006). Rediscovering the juvenile justice ideal in the United States. In J. Muncie and B. Goldson (Eds.), *Comparative youth justice: critical issues*. (pp. 6-18) London: Sage Publications.

Lakes, R. D. (1994). Introduction: Critical education for work. In R. D. Lakes (Ed.), *Critical education for work: Multidisciplinary approaches* (pp. 1 – 16). Norwood, NJ: Ablex Publishing.

Lahm, K. (2010). Equal or equitable: An exploration of educational and vocational program availability for male and female offenders. In E. Latessa and A. Holsinger (Eds.), *Correctional contexts: Contemporary and classical readings* (pp.278-289). New York: Oxford University Press.

LeBel, T. (2009). Formerly incarcerated persons' use of advocacy/activism as a coping orientation in the reintegration process. In B. M. Veysey, J. Christian, & D. J. Martinez (Eds.), *How offenders transform their lives.* (pp. 165-187). Portland, OR: Willan Publishing.

Lee, B. Rep. (2007). Congressional black caucus. *Congressional Record.* (House of Representatives - July 23, 2007) Page: H8283.

Lembert, L. B., Bergeron, S. and Linker, M. (2005). Negotiating the politics of space: Teaching women's studies in a women's prison. *NWSA Journal,* 17 (2) 199 – 208.

Lewis, J. (1998). *Walking the wind: A memoir of the movement.* New York: Harcourt Brace and Co.

Linebaugh, P. (1995). Freeing birds erasing images, burning lamps: How I learned to teach in prison. In H. S. Davidson (Ed.), *Schooling in a "total institution": Critical perspectives on prison education* (pp. 65-90). Westport, CT: Bergin and Garvey.

Linton, J. (2005). United States Department of Education update. *The Journal of Correctional Education,* 56 (2) 90 – 95.

Lipman, P. (2007). "No Child Left Behind:" Globalization, privatization, and the politics of inequality. In E. Ross and R.Gibson (Eds.), *Neoliberalism and education reform* (pp.35-58). Cresskill, NJ: Hampton Press.

Livingstone, D.W. (1997). The limits of human capital theory: Expanding knowledge, informal learning and underemployment. *Policy Options,* July/August. P. 9.

MacLeavy, J. (2006). The language of politics and the politics of language: Unpacking 'social exclusion' in New Labour policy. *Space and Polity,* (10) 1, 87-98.

Mageehon, A. (2008). *Value, belief and experience in women's jail-based adult education.* Bethesda, MD: Academica Press.

Marable, M. (1999). Mastering the art of Black male prisoner education. *Black Issues in Higher Education,* 16 (15) 80.

Maruna, S. and LeBel, T. (2010). Welcome home? Examining the "reentry court" concept from a strength-based perspective. In E. Latessa and A. Holsinger (Eds.), *Correctional contexts: Contemporary and classical readings* (pp.324-344). New York: Oxford University Press.

Mauer, M. (2006). *Race to incarcerate.* New York: The New Press.

Mattuci, R. and Johnson, M. (2003). Teaching hands – on plumbing in a county facility: A working plumber's experience. *The Journal of Correctional Education,* 54 (1) 15 –18.

McCaffrey, S. (2007). Aging Inmates Clogging Nation's Prisons: Prisons Face Growing Population of Elderly Inmates, Rising Health Costs. *ABC News Internet Ventures.* Retrieved September 30, 2007 from http://abcnews. go.com/print?id+3669712

Meiners, E. (2007). *Right to be hostile: Schools, prisons, and the making of public enemies.* New York: Routledge.

Mfume, K. Rep (1994). Personal explanation. *Congressional Record* (House of Representatives - August 21, 1994) Page: H9000.

Milner, A., & Browitt, J. (2002). *Contemporary cultural theory: An introduction.* London: Routledge.

Moore, G. Rep. (2007). Second chance act of 2007. *Congressional Record.* (House of Representatives - November 13, 2007) Page: H 13579.

Morse, J. (2002). In the shadow of the thirteenth amendment. In B. Gaucher (Ed.), *Writing as resistance: Journal of prisoners on prisons anthology (1988- 2002)* (pp. 127-150). Toronto, Ontario: Canadian Scholar's Press.

Muccoaroni, G. & Quirk, P. (2006). *Deliberative choices: Debating public policy in congress.* Chicago: University of Chicago Press.

Muhlhausen, D. (2011). The second chance act: Strengthening safe and effective community re-entry. *U.S. Government Printing Office.* (U.S. Senate – July, 21, 2010). Retrieved May 1, 2011 from http:// www.gpo.gov/fdsys/pkg/CHRG-111shrg64378/pdf/CHRG-111shrg64 378.pdf.

Mumola, C. J. (2000). Incarcerated parents and their children. *Bureau of Justice Statistics, Special Report*. NCJ 182335. Washington, DC: U.S. Department of Justice, Bureau of Justice Statistics.

Muncie, J. & Godson, B. (2006). States of transition: Convergence and diversity international youth justice. In J. Muncie and B. Godson (Eds.), *Comparative youth justice* (pp. 196 - 218). London: Sage Publications.

Navarro, V. (2002). Neoliberalism, "globalization," unemployment, inequalities, and the welfare state. In V. Navarro (Ed.), *The political economy of social inequalities: Consequences for health and quality of life*. (pp. 33 - 108). Amityville, NJ: Baywood Publishing.

Obama, B. Sen. (2005). The second chance act. *Congressional Record* (Senate – November 08, 2005) Page: S12521.

O'Hear, M. (2007). The second chance act and the future of the reentry movement. *Marquette University Law School Legal Studies Research Paper Series*. Research Paper No. 07-15. Retrieved May 3, 2008 from http://ssrn.com/abstract=1077278.

Olguin, B. (2010). *La pinta: Chicana/o prisoner literature, culture, and politics*. Austin: University of Texas Press.

Oliver, W. M. (2003). *The law and order presidency*. Upper Saddle River, NJ: Prentice Hall.

Osgerby, B. (2002). "A caste, a culture, a market:" Youth, marketing, and lifestyle in postwar America. In R. Strickland (Ed.), *Growing up postmodern: Neoliberalism and the war on the young*. (pp. 15-34). Lanham, MA: Rowman and Littlefield.

Owens, M. Rep. (1992). Higher education amendments of 1992. *Congressional Record* (House of Representatives - March 26, 1992) Page: H1896.

Palumbo, D. (1988). *Public policy in America: Government in action*. San Diego, CA: Harcourt Brace Jovanovich Publishers.

Page, J. (2004). Eliminating the enemy: The import of denying prisoners access to higher education in Clinton's America. *Punishment and Society*, 6 (4) 357 – 378.

Pavis, R. (2002). Preparing federal prison inmates for employment after release: An intervention at the Federal Bureau of Prisons. *The Journal of Correctional Education*, 53 (4) 146 – 149.

Peck, J. & Tickell, A. (2007). Conceptualizing neoliberalism, thinking Thatcherism. In H. Leitner, J. Peck, E. Sheppard (Eds.), *Contesting neoliberalism: Urban frontiers* (pp. 26-50). New York: The Guilford Press.

Pell, C. Sen. (1993). Violent crime control and law enforcement act of 1993. *Congressional Record* (Senate - November 17, 1993) Page: S15967.

Pell, C. Sen. (1994). Two articles from the Washington Post on corrections education. *Congressional Record* (Senate – February 09, 1994) Page: S1275.

Perkinson, R. (2010). *Texas tough: The rise of America's prison empire.* New York: Metropolitan Books.

Petersilia, J. (2011). Beyond the prison bubble. *Wilson Quarterly,* 35 (1) pp. 50-55.

Phillips, J. (2000). *Contested knowledge: A guide to critical theory.* London: Zed Books.

Piven, F. F., & Cloward, R. A. (1983). Humanitarianism in history: A response to the critics. In W. I. Trattner (Ed.), *Social welfare or social control? Some reflections on regulating the poor* (pp. 114 -148). Knoxville, TN: The University of Tennessee Press.

Potter, G. W. & Kappeler, V. E. (2006). *Constructing crime: Perspectives on making news and social problems* (2nd ed.). Long Grove: Waveland Press, Inc.

Pompa, L. (2011). Breaking down the walls: Inside-out learning and the pedagogy of transformation. In S. Hartnett (Ed.), *Challenging the prison-industrial complex: Activism, arts and educational alternatives* (pp. 253-272). Urbana, IL: University of Illinois Press.

Rangel, C. Rep. (2006). Expungement restores most fundamentals rights. *Congressional Record* (Extensions of Remarks - March 01, 2006) Page: E237.

Rangel, C. Rep. (2007). Encourage community safety through recidivism prevention. *Congressional Record* (Extensions of Remarks - July 13, 2007) Page: E1506.

Reinarman, C. & Duskin, C. (2006). Dominant ideology and drugs in the media. In G. W. Potter and V. E. Kappeler (Eds.), *Constructing crime: Perspectives on making news and social problems* (pp. 331 – 344). Long Grove, IL: Waveland Press, Inc.

Reeves, J. (1994). *Cracked coverage: Television news, the anti-cocaine crusade, and the Reagan legacy.* Durham, NC: Duke University Press.

Reich, A. (2010). *Hidden truth: Young men navigating lives in and out of juvenile prison.* Berkeley: University of California Press.

Rivera, J. A. (1995). A nontraditional approach to social and criminal justice. In H. S. Davidson (Ed.), *Schooling in a "total institution": Critical perspectives on prison education* (pp. 159 – 172).Westport, CT: Bergin and Garvey.

Ruddell, R. (2004). *America behind bars: Trends in imprisonment:1950-2000.* New York: LFB Scholarly Publishing LLC.

Rush, F. (2004). Conceptual foundations of early critical theory. In F. Rush (Ed.), *The Cambridge companion to critical theory* (pp. 6 – 39). Cambridge, UK: Cambridge University Press.

Sabol, W. J. & Cuture, H. (2008). Prison inmates at midyear 2007. *Bureau of Justice Statistics, Special Report,* NCJ 221944. Washington, DC: U.S. Department of Justice, Bureau of Justice Statistics.

Saks, P. (2007). *Tearing down the walls: confronting the class divide in American education.* Berkeley: University of California Press.

Sahlins, M. (1972). *Stone age economics.* London: Tavistock.

Santos, M. (2006). *Inside: Life behind bars in America.* New York: St. Martin's Press.

Sasson, T. (1995) *Crime talk: How citizens construct a social problem.* Hawthorne, NY: Aldine De Gruyter.

Sassone, L. A. (2000). Individualization. In D. A. Gabbard (Ed.), *Knowledge and power in the global economy: Politics and the rhetoric of school reform.* (pp. 389 - 392). Mahwah, NJ: Lawrence Erlbaum Associates, Inc.

Schenet M., Powner, D., Stedman, J. & Shohov, T. (2003). *Pell grants: Background and issues.* New York: Novinka Books.

Schiffren, D., Tannen, D. & Hamilton, H. (2001). Contributors. In D. Schiffren, D. Tannen, H.Hamilton (Eds.), *The handbook of discourse analysis* (p. x). Malden, MA: Blackwell Publishers.

Schmidt, B. (2008). Rich/poor income gap widening to chasm. *CBS News.* Retrieved May 3, 2008 from http://www.cbsnews.com/stories/2008 /05/03/earlyshow/living/money/printable4068795 .shtml.

Scott, R. Rep. (2005). The second chance act. *Congressional Record* (House of Representatives - December 06, 2005) Page: H11095.

Scott, R. Rep. (2011). Reauthorization of the second chance act hearing. *U.S Government Printing Office.* (House of Representatives - September 29, 2010) Retrieved May 3, 2011 from http://www.gpo.gov/fdsys/pkg/CHRG-111hhrg58479/pdf/ CHRG –111hhrg58479.pdf.

Scott, R. Rep. (2009). The introduction of the youth promise act. *Congressional Record* (House of Representatives -February 13, 2009) Page: E285.

Second Chance Act of 2005. Hearing before the subcommittee on crime, terrorism, and homeland security of the committee of the judiciary. House of Representatives. *Congressional Record.* 109th Congress (2005).

Second Chance Act of 2007. H.R. 1593. *Congressional Record.* (House of Representatives - November 13, 2007) Page: H13570.

Second Chance Act of 2007. H.R. 1593.*Congressional Record.* (House of Representatives. November 13, 2007) Page: H13572.

Second Chance Act of 2007. H.R. 1593 *Congressional Record.* (House of Representatives- November 13, 2007). Page: H13573.

Segall, W. (2006). *School reform in a global society.* Lanham, MA: Rowman and Littlefield Publishers.

Selman, D. & Leighton, P. (2010). *Punishment for sale: Private prisons, big business, and the incarceration binge.* Lanham, MD: Rowman & Littlefield Publishers.

Sexton, J. (2007). Racial profiling and the societies of control. In J. James (Ed.), *Warfare in the American homeland: Policing and prison in a penal democracy* (pp. 197 – 218). Durham, NC: Duke University Press.

Seymour, C. (2001). Children with parents in prison: Child welfare policy, program, and practice issues. In C. Seymour and C.Hairston (Eds.), *Children with parents in prison* (pp. 1 – 26). New Brunswick: Transaction Publishers.

Sidanius, J. & Pratto, F. (1999). *Social dominance: An intergroup theory of social hierarchy and oppression.* Cambridge, UK: Cambridge University Press.

Simmons, C. W. (2003). California law and the children of prisoners. *California Research Bureau,* California State Library.

Simon, R., Dippo, D. & Sheaker, A. (1991). Learning work: A critical pedagogy of work education. Westport, CT: Bergin and Garvey.

Simon, R. (1991). *Gramsci's political thought: An introduction.* London: Lawrence and Wishart.

Singh, R. (1998). *The Congressional Black Caucus: Racial Politics in the U.S. Congress.* Thousand Oaks, CA: Sage Publications, Inc.

Sharp, E. (2010). On the border: Faith-based initiatives and Pentecostal praxis in Brownsville, Texas. In J. Adkins, L. Occhipinti, T. Hefferan (Eds.), *Not by faith alone: Social services, social justice, and faith-based organizations in the United States.* (pp. 51 – 67). Lanham, MD: Lexington Books.

Sokoloff, N. (2007). The effect of the prison-industrial complex on African American women. In M. Marable, I. Steinberg and K. Middlemass (Eds.), *Racializing justice, disenfranchising lives: The racism, criminal justice and law reader* (pp. 73 - 90). New York: Palgrave Macmillan.

Sparks, R. (2003). State punishment in advanced capitalist countries. In T. G. Blomberg & S. Cohen (Eds.), *Punishment and social control* (pp. 19 - 44). New York: Aldine De Gruyter.

Specter, A. Sen. (1989). Statements on introduced bills and joint resolutions. *Congressional Record* (Senate - April 11, 1989) Page: S3626.

Specter, A. Sen. (2004). Statements on introduced bills and joint resolutions. *Congressional Record* (Senate - October 07, 2004) Page: S10724.

Specter, A. Sen. (2008). Passage of the second chance act. *Congressional Record* (Senate - March 12, 2008). Page: S1993.

Spierenburg, P.C. (2010). The spectacle of suffering. In E. Latessa and A. Holsinger (Eds.), *Correctional contexts: Contemporary and classical readings* (pp.4-16). New York: Oxford University Press.

Spring, J. (2000). Choice. In D. Gabbard (Ed.), *Knowledge and power in the global economy: Politics and the rhetoric of school reform* (pp. 25 - 32). Mahwah, NJ: Lawrence Erlbaum Associates.

State of the Union Address. (2004, January 20).*Whitehouse.gov.* Retrieved January 9, 2009, from http://www.whitehouse.gov/news/releases/2004/01/print/ 20040120-7.html.

Steiner, J. (2001). Institutional challenges in pedagogy. In J. Daly, P.Schall, R. Steele (Eds.), *Protecting the right to teach children: Power, politics and public schools* (pp.153 –170). New York, NY: Teachers College Press.

Stern, V. (2006). Mr. Bush and neoliberalism. In R. Robison (Ed.), *The neoliberal revolution in: Forging the market state* (pp. 173 - 194). New York: Palgrave Macmillan.

Steuer, S. J. (2001). Historical development of a model for correctional educational literacy. *The Journal of Correctional Education.* 52 (2) 48 – 51.

Stephey, M. J. (2007). De-criminalizing mental illness. *Time Magazine.* Downloaded August 13, 2007 from http://www.time.com/time/printout/0,8816,1651002,00.html.

Stoddard, E. & Cornwall, G. (2001). The future of liberal education and the hegemony of market values: Privilege, practicality and citizenship. *Liberal Education.* June 22, 2001. 87:3. Retrieved April 23,2009 from www.thefreelibrary.com.

Street, P. (2003). Color bind. In T. Herivel and P. Wright (Eds.), *Prison nation: The warehousing of the nation's poor* (pp. 30 – 40). New York: Routledge.

Sweeney, M. (2010). *Reading is my window: Books and the art of reading in women's prisons.* Chapel Hill: University of North Carolina Press.

Tabb, W. K. (2006). Mr. Bush and neoliberalism. In R. Robinsin (Ed.), *Neoliberal revolution: Forging the market state.* New York: Palgrave MacMillan.

Taylor, J. M. (2005). Alternative funding options for post-secondary correctional education. *Journal of Correctional Education,* 56 (1) 6, 12.

Teeple, G. & McBride, S. (2011). Global crisis and political economy. In G. Teeple & S. McBride (Eds.), *Relations of global power: Neoliberal order and disorder* (pp. ix-xix). Toronto: University of Toronto Press.

Thompson, K. (1998). *Moral panics.* London: Routledge.

Thompson, M. & Cummings, D. (2010). Enhancing the career development of individuals who have criminal records. *The Career Development Quarterly,* 58 (209 - 218).

Tonry, M. (2002). Racial politics, radical disparities and the war on crime. In C. Reasons, D.Conley and J. Debro (Eds.), *Race, class, gender and justice in the United States* (pp. 71 - 84). Boston, MA: Allyn and Bacon.

Toor, R. (October 25, 2010). Teaching in the pokey. *The Chronicle of Higher Education.* Retrieved March 18, 2011 from http://chronicle.com/ article/ Teaching-in -the-Pokey/125065/.

Towns E. Rep. (1994). Amendments offered by Mr. Hunter. *Congressional Record* (House of Representatives - April 20, 1994) Page: H2547.

Travis, T., McBride, E. C. & Solomon, A. L. (2005). Families left behind: *The hidden costs of incarceration and reentry*. Washington, DC: Urban Institute.

Tubbs-Jones, S. Rep. (2005) The second chance act. *Congressional Record* (House of Representatives - December 06, 2005) Page: H11095.

Tubbs Jones, S. Rep. (2007). Second chance act. *Congressional Record* (House of Representatives - July 23, 2007) Page: H8283.

Tubbs Jones, S. Rep. (2007). Second chance act of 2007. *Congressional Record* (House of Representatives - November 13, 2007) Page: H13579.

2009 Criminal Justice Coalition (2009) Smart on crime: Recommendations for the next administration and congress. *Criminal Justice Coalition*. Retrieved from http://2009transition.org/criminaljustice/index.php?option=com_content&view=article&id=70&Itemid=40

Ubah, C. B. (2002). A critical examination of empirical studies of offender rehabilitation—correctional education: Lessons for the 21st century. *The Journal of Correctional Education*, 53(1), 13-19.

Ubah, C. B. (2004). Abolition of Pell grants for higher education of prisoners: Examining antecedents and consequences. *Journal of Offender Rehabilitation*. 39 (2), 73 - 85.

U.S. Department of Education (2004). Student financial aid. *U.S. Department of Education*. Retrieved December 3, 2008 from http://www.ifap.ed.gov/sfahandbooks/attachments/0304Vol3Ch1.pdf.

U.S. Department of Education (2009). Partnerships between community colleges and prisons: providing workforce education and training to reduce recidivism. U.S. Department of Education Washington, D.C.: *U.S. Department of Education*. Retrieved March 17, 2011 from http://www2.ed.gov/about/offices/list/ovae/pi/AdultEd/prison-cc-partnerships_2009.pdf

U.S. Department of Justice (2008). In a 15 state study over two-thirds of released prisoners were rearrested within three years. *Bureau of Justice Statistics*. Retrieved September 3, 2008 from http://www.ojp.usdoj gov/bjs/reentry/recidivism.htm.

Valentine, K. B. (1998). "If the guards only knew": Communication education for women in prison. *Women's Studies in Communication*, 21 (2) 238 – 244.

van Dijk, T.A. (1987). *Communicating racism: Ethnic prejudice in thought and talk*. Newbury Park, CA: Sage Publications.

van Dijk, T.A. (1993). *Elite discourse and racism*. Newbury Park, CA: Sage Publications.

van Dijk, T.A. (2001). Critical discourse analysis. In D. Schiffren, D. Tannen, H. Hamilton (Eds.), *The handbook of discourse analysis* (p. 352-371). Malden, MA: Blackwell Publishers.

Vile, M. C. (2007). *Politics in the USA* (6th ed.). New York:Routledge.

Wacquant, L. (1999). Urban marginality in the coming millennium. *Urban studies*, 36 (10) 1639 - 1647.

Wacquant, L. (2001). The penalisation of poverty and the rise of neoliberalism. *European journal on criminal policy and research*, 9 (4) 401-412.

Wacquant, L. (2008). *Urban outcasts: A comparative sociology of advanced marginality*. Malden, MA: Polity Press.

Walmsley R. (2009) World Prison Population List 8th ed.*International Centre for Prison Studies*: London. Retrieved February 22, 2011 from http://www.kcl.ac.uk/depsta/law/research/icps/downloads/ wppl-8th_41.pdf.

Warner, K. & Gehring, T. (2007). Against the narrowing of perspectives: How do we see learning, prisons and prisoners? *Journal of Correctional Education*, 58 (2) 170 – 185.

Warren, J. (2008). *One in 100: Behind bars in 2008*. Washington, DC: The Pew Charitable Trust.

Weigel, G. (1996). Christian conviction and democratic etiquette. In M. Gerson (Ed.), *The essential neoconservative reader* (pp. 395 –410). Reading, M.A.: Perseus Publishing.

Welch, M. (1996). *Corrections: A critical approach*. New York: McGraw-Hill.

Welch, M. (2011). *Corrections: A critical approach*. New York: Routledge.

Western, B. and Becket, K. (1999). How unregulated is the U.S. labor market? The penal system as a labor market institution. *American Journal of Sociology*, 104 (4) 1030 – 1060.

Will, G. (1994). Two articles from the washington post on corrections education. *Congressional Record*. (Senate - February 09, 1994).Page: S1276.

Wilson, J. (2001). Political discourse. In D. Schiffren, D. Tannen, H. Hamilton (Eds.), *The handbook of discourse analysis* (pp. 398-415). Malden, MA: Blackwell Publishers.

Wineburg, B. (2007). *Faith-based inefficiency*. Westport: Praeger Publishers.

Wodak, R., de Cillia, R., Reisigl, M. & Liebhart, K. (1999). *The discourse construction of national identity. Edinburgh:* Edinburgh University Press.

Wodak, R., & Chilton, P. (2005). Interdisciplinarity and critical discourse analysis. In R.Wodak, and P. Chilton (Eds.), *A new agenda in (critical) discourse analysis.* Amsterdam: John Benjamins Publishing Company.

Wood, L., & Kroger, W. (2000). *Doing discourse analysis: Methods for studying action in talk and text.* Thousand Oaks, CA: Sage Publications.

Woods, N. (2006). *Describing discourse: A practical guide to discourse analysis.* London: Oxford University Press.

Wright, M. (2001). Pell grants, politics and the penitentiary: Connections between the development of U.S. higher education and prisoner post-secondary programs. *The Journal of Correctional Education,* 52 (1) 11 – 15.

Young, D. & Mattuci, R. (2006). Enhancing the vocational skills of incarcerated women through a plumbing maintenance program. *The Journal of Correctional Education,* 57 (2) 126 – 140.

Zook, J. (1994, August 10). Crime bill would bar Pell grants to federal and state prisoners. *The Chronicle of Higher Education,* A 24.

Index